Rediscovering the Heart of God

First Century Faith.   The Spark of Revival.

Graeme McLiesh

Rediscovering the Heart of God

Author: Graeme McLiesh

Editor: Lee Thomas

Cover: Graeme McLiesh and designlhbsbd

ISBN: 979-8358761377

Imprint: Independently published by The heart of prophecy.

email contact: theheartofprophecy.com

Contents

Preface

I want to thank everyone for buying this book. It has taken more than two years to write and your support is appreciated. I understand that the ideas in this book are not commonly understood in the church and I am excited to reveal the blessings that come with Hebrew thinking.

I wish to acknowledge and appreciate the help I have had. I firstly want to thank Lee Thomas in the USA for her consistent encouragement. Also my friends at Fire church in Melbourne such as Kieron Lane, Carmen Standfield and Linda Harvey. I have had other friends too like Tania Narva and Helen Lord who have been very generous with their encouragement. Writing this book has not been an easy task. I also want to thank Brian Simmons for providing me with his insightful review.

It is my hope that as time goes by more people will come to understand the Hebrew way of thinking and the profound impact that it can have. For those looking to explore these ideas further feel free to send an email to info@theheartofprophecy.com. It is my plan to write more books in the future and develop seminars and online training. I also hope to set up a newsletter. These will be designed with a view to communicating a deeper understanding of Hebrew thinking as well as how to develop greater intimacy with God.

Be Blessed
Graeme McLiesh
October 14, 2022.

Chapter One

Introduction

Jesus founded a movement that is currently estimated to have more than two billion followers. Jesus is respected and idolised by countless people, and this includes many who would not even describe themselves as Christian. Despite all this adulation, very few preach like him. Despite his personal significance, Jesus' style of preaching is ignored almost universally. People ask, "What would Jesus do?" But it seems few are asking, "What would Jesus say? "Before we seek to answer this question, let's look at John 5:19.

John 5:19 Then Jesus answered and said to them, "Most assuredly, I say to you, the Son can do nothing of Himself, but what He sees the Father do; for whatever He does, the Son also does in like manner. NKJV

In John 5:19, there is a clear statement that everything Jesus did was approved and directed by his Heavenly Father. This must include the way Jesus preached. There is a disconnect here that seems glaringly obvious. The question is why? Paul spoke at some length about the issues that underlie this disconnect and is essentially saying we should think more like Jesus. But teaching this emphasis is rare, much less thought to have any relevance to homiletics (the study of preaching). St John, especially in his epistles, speaks strongly against the underlying cause of this disconnect. This disconnect actually points to a broader range of issues with significant implications. Most theologians agree that Greek thinking has come to determine the way the church looks at Scripture.

When we think from a Greek perspective, we start with the premise that man is at the centre of all things. The Hebrew perspective starts with the premise that God is at the centre of all things. The Greek mind seeks to understand God by approaching Him using our minds and logical deduction. Alternatively, the Hebrew mind seeks to understand God by faith and revelation. (1) Therefore, Greek thinking defines the way churches teach people to approach God. Later in this book (chapter 12), it will be shown that the way Jesus preached comes directly from his Hebrew values. The Hebrew and Greek approaches to thought are connected to contrasting values and approaches to life. One reason that the academic world adopted the Greek approach, and has largely ignored the Hebrew approach, is that Greek is the language of intellectualism (as discussed in chapter 7).

There is a key point of difference between Greek and Hebrew thinking. This key difference is that Greek thinking seeks to find answers from the human intellect whereas Hebrew thinking seeks to find answers from the human spirit and the presence of God. This book is written as a guide to help people explore the meaning of Scripture. The desired end result is that it will enable readers to be more spiritual, as well as increase their level of intimacy with God. If we seek to approach God like a Hebrew thinker we must explore issues of intimacy and relationship with God. In addition, we must leave behind the intellectualisation of our faith that was introduced by Greek thinking.

In chapter 11 of this book, the Hebrew language and Hebrew thinking are examined. Then it will provide examples of where Hebrew thinking brings significantly different perspectives than the Greek language and thinking. Not only does this book discuss the preaching style of Jesus in chapter 13, it also explores the way Paul approaches the differences between Hebrew and Greek thought. It will be argued that both Jesus and Paul approached their belief systems from a Hebrew perspective. In addition, they both rejected the Greek approach in significant teachings about spirituality. John also wrote from this perspective (refer to chapter 14).

In this book, the history of Greek influence will be examined, and the consequences of Greek thought will be explored (refer to Chapter 7). This book argues these consequences are extremely significant, and if the main premise of this book is true, then much of the church is approaching God in a way that is fundamentally unbiblical. For anyone who is serious about their relationship with God, these are critical issues.

In this modern world, our academic institutions are based on Greek philosophy and thinking. Greek thinking has provided the model for the mindset of the western world. This mindset defines the way most modern people view the world. The influence of Greek thinking is so pervasive that those who live in our modern culture are typically unaware of the Greek philosophical influence. However, this influence underpins every aspect of our modern lifestyle. Greek thinking brings with it a complete mindset that puts a priority on academic thinking and embodies the general values of Greek philosophy. This mindset is discussed in multiple chapters. The Greek language is the language of The Greek New Testament and the Septuagint. This is the Greek translation of the Hebrew Old Testament and was written between 250 and 150 BC. These translations came about at the request of Ptolemy II, a Greek Egyptian Pharaoh. They reflect the influence of Greek culture at that time, an influence that was strong even within the Roman Empire.

The transition from Hebrew thinking to Greek thinking can be traced back to the first four centuries of the church (refer to chapter 7). Some of the strongest support for Greek thinking is provided by Saint Augustine (356-430 AD). St. Augustine is considered by many to be the greatest of the church fathers. Central to his theology was an integration of the philosophical influences of Plato and Neo-Platonism with the gospel.

Diarmaid MacCulloch, a historian, has written, "Augustine's impact on Western Christian thought can hardly be overstated; only his beloved example, Paul of Tarsus, has been more influential, and Westerners have generally seen Paul through Augustine's eyes." (2) The influence of Augustine and Aquinas plus a range of other early Christian thinkers have been influential in leading today's churches to interpret biblical values through the lens of Greek thought. This is especially true in the realm of academic theology. While Diarmaid MacCulloch's statement may be true, " Westerners have generally seen Paul through Augustine's eyes." (3) The larger truth is, with rare exceptions. the whole of the Christian faith has been seen through the eyes of Augustine.

Most Christian academics accept this Greek influence and have chosen to endorse Augustine's interpretation of the faith (as discussed in chapter 10). The fact that the church changed its thinking from the days of the early apostles to Greek thinking is generally agreed upon. Most academics seem to argue that the differences between Greek and Hebrew thought are insignificant. In addition, believers seem to be unaware that a disconnect exists. Hebrew thought was native to the human authors of every Old Testament book except Ruth. The New Testament is thought of as being written in Greek and this Greek text is what our translations are based on. However, every author, except for Luke, came from a Hebrew background, and there is evidence to indicate there was a very strong Hebrew influence within the New Testament. In New Testament times the language of Rabbinic discussion was most definitely Hebrew. Jesus and his disciples would have mainly spoken to each other in Hebrew and Aramaic.

The Hebrew mindset is vastly different from the Greek mindset. This is discussed further in chapter 6. It is the purpose of this book to show that the influence of Greek thinking and language on the church is not the innocuous influence that some have argued it to be. The Greek influence on biblical scholarship has led to distortions in the actual message that is presented in today's churches. Embedded in the ideas of today's Christian church are many values that are foreign to Hebrew thinking. It is argued when people seek to live a "biblical" life, yet do so through the lens of Greek thinking this concept of "biblical" is distorted. Ultimately, this process means the concept of being "biblical" is understood to be something it is simply not (4).

Virtually all churches claim that their practices and theology are "biblical". A range of churches including those influenced by Calvinism, seek to follow the principle of Sola Scriptura. This is

Latin for "by Scripture alone". The evangelical church movement is based on the concept of being loyal to the Scriptural revelation of Jesus. in addition, typical churches in the Pentecostal and Charismatic movements seek to be Biblical.

The purpose of this book is to help readers discover the values and approach that comes when we re-examine the lessons of Hebrew thinking. In addition, this book is written to help readers understand the values of Greek thinking. These are values that exist today and are not seriously challenged in most churches. These are serious issues. The contention of this book is that when they are understood, some profound messages and values embedded in Scripture will be revealed. This is despite the fact that these messages have been largely ignored. Like the proverbial iceberg, the tips of these values may be apparent, but there is much greater meaning below the surface.

This book is anything but a criticism of the Bible. In fact, this book has been written as an exploration of the original intentions of the Bible's authors. If we can touch the divine inspiration of Scripture, that would be even better. Simply put, the goal of this book is that true biblical values will be better understood and hopefully practised.

The basic thesis of this book is that Greek philosophy was not the positive source of inspiration that many church leaders and academics have seen it to be. Instead, this book argues that the Greek language and thinking have influenced many contemporary church practices influencing them to be at odds with the original heart and intent of the Scriptures. There are many ways that modern Christians seek to express their faith within the church, and many of these have been developed from a Greek thinking perspective. This means these practices significantly vary from the Hebrew heart of Scripture. It is more than disappointing that many believers with the best intentions, as well as a genuine desire to be truly biblical, have followed this path. The result is a set of values at cross purposes to the original intent of the Bible. This book seeks to challenge these norms and help people understand what is truly biblical, as this is what a Hebrew perspective reveals.

Chapter Two

The Danger of Syncretism

When the first General Secretary of the World Council of Churches was asked to name the greatest danger peril facing the church, he replied: "Syncretism. It is a far more dangerous challenge to the Christian church than atheism will ever be." (5)

The Cambridge dictionary describes syncretism as "the combining of different religions, cultures, or ideas". (6) Syncretism does not necessarily involve the denial of any biblical doctrine but involves the addition of ideas that are derived from foreign beliefs. Our opening quote asserts that the compromise of syncretism is dangerous. This compromise is far from new. The book of Colossians was written in the context of syncretism coming from false teachers of that age. These teachers were seeking to combine the pure gospel with ideas originating from Judaism and early versions of Gnosticism. For further discussion on Gnosticism refer to 6.8. As a response to this, Paul writes in Colossians 1:28 that all wisdom is found in Jesus and not a religious system or philosophy.

Colossians 1:28 Him we preach, warning every man and teaching every man in all wisdom, that we may present every man perfect in Christ Jesus. NKJV

Isaiah writes of the syncretism and compromise of the house of Jacob in Isaiah 2:6 and 8.

Isaiah 2:6 For You have forsaken Your people, the house of Jacob,

Because they are filled with eastern ways;

They are soothsayers like the Philistines,

And they are pleased with the children of foreigners.

.. 8 Their land is also full of idols;

They worship the work of their own hands,

That which their own fingers have made. NKJV

When we read contemporary commentaries on the problem of syncretism, some like Mark Rushdoony identify the problem of ecumenism as being the main source of the problem. This is where biblical principles are compromised for the sake of church "unity". He also cites the problem of what he describes as "seeker-sensitive churches" that seek to present a positive rather than a biblical message. (7)

Most writers, however, seem to find the greatest threat from syncretism comes from compromises made on the mission field. (8)(9) An example of this can be found in Charles Kraft's description of his experience as a missionary. (10) When Charles and his wife started their mission experience in Nigeria, their theology was typically Evangelical. They were well prepared when they arrived as they had studied the language and the culture as well as theology. They found that despite all this, the priority of their Nigerian church was their interaction with the spiritual world. This was something Kraft was unprepared for. The Nigerians would regularly discuss a wide range of problems that they claimed were caused by evil spirits.

The leaders of the Nigerian church sought to teach about the authority of Jesus in the spiritual realm. Despite Kraft's inexperience in approaching this kind of spirituality, the Nigerians told him that he was more open to understanding it than his missionary colleagues. The Nigerian leaders would regularly preach that the power of God was capable of healing and delivering people from demonic oppression, yet these leaders were unable to demonstrate this power. As a consequence, the locals were left unimpressed by these claims. The missionaries were seen as bringing a powerless message to a people whose focus was power. That is not to say the Christian message had no relevance. Many Nigerians embraced the Christian message of love, forgiveness and acceptance, however, the lack of power meant that many of the Nigerians had deep spiritual needs that were left unmet. This disconnect opened the door for syncretism. The locals continued to follow traditional pagan practices in order to meet their power needs. While the missionaries were critical of this practice, it was to no avail. The temptation towards syncretism is common where traditional religions are seen to provide solutions that are unavailable to the Christian witness. (11)

This is a dangerous phenomenon, and the church is generally vigilant in the way it protects itself from forms of syncretism like pagan practices. It is the core thesis of this book that there is a far more insidious form of syncretism that can be found inside the church. This syncretism has found its place and has been largely unnoticed and unidentified.

Chapter Three

The Issue of Deception

P art of the premise of this book is that syncretism has come into the church. The universality of Greek-style thinking has meant that with very few exceptions everyone in the Western world is trained in Greek thinking. I intend to show in this book that this Greek thinking approach leads to deception when it comes to thinking about the things of God. This book is arguing that there has been deception that has come against the church and the elect of God. This premise will no doubt be contentious for some and raise many questions. Firstly, is this deception something that is consistent with what is written in Scripture? Secondly, how is it possible that such deception exists? This chapter seeks to answer the first question fully and provides a framework for answering the second. (12) Deception is something that the Bible mentions multiple times, and according to Matthew 24:24, even God's elect needs to be careful. In 2 Corinthians 4:4, Paul writes about how the god of this world has blinded the minds of those who don't believe and Ephesians 2:2 speaks of how Satan is at work in the disobedient.1 Corinthians 1:20 Where is the wise man (philosopher)? Where is the scribe (scholar)? Where is the debater (logician, orator) of this age? Has God not exposed the foolishness of this world's wisdom? AMP. The Holy Spirit leads us in all truth. This specific account of deception can be found in 1 John 2 and the verses that first discuss this issue can be found in 1 John 2 18. There is a further discussion on the significance of these verses especially 1 John 4:1-3 in chapter 15. Along with the idea that the spirit is good and material is evil come many deceptions. A few more include:

In section 3.1 you will read about biblical warnings against deception. These relate to a threat that was urgent, not something future and distant. Jesus' warning in Matthew 7:15 was written in the present tense, The warning in 2 Peter 2:1 can be dated at 66AD and was written in the future tense. The warning of 1 John, estimated to be written 25 years later, is describing events that were already happening. The events recorded in I John 2 and 4 can be understood as Peter's prophecy starting to be fulfilled.

3.1 Biblical warnings against Deception.

Matthew 24:24 For false Christs and false prophets will appear and they will provide great signs and wonders, so as to deceive, if possible, even the elect (God's chosen ones). AMP

As it says in Hosea, God's people were destroyed for lack of knowledge.

Hosea 4:6 My people are destroyed for lack of knowledge. Because you have rejected knowledge, I also will reject you from being priest for Me; Because you have forgotten the law of your God, I also will forget your children. NKJV.

Of all the things in life we must understand, deception has to be very important. The warning Jesus gave in Matthew 24:4 was given when the disciples spoke to Jesus privately on the Mount of Olives. Even the disciples were warned to be careful about being misled. Matthew 24:5 says that many will be misled. Matthew 24:11 says false prophets will mislead many. So the idea that it is dangerous to be complacent about the possibility of deception is a biblical one.

Matthew 24:3 While Jesus was seated on the Mount of Olives, the disciples came to Him privately, and said, "Tell us, when will this [destruction of the temple] take place, and what will be the sign of Your coming, and of the end (completion, consummation) of the age?" 4 Jesus answered, "Be careful that no one misleads you [deceiving you and leading you into error]. 5 For many will come in My name [misusing it, and appropriating the strength of the name which belongs to Me], saying, 'I am the Christ (the Messiah, the Anointed),' and they will mislead many. AMP

Mat 24:11 Many false prophets will appear and mislead many. AMP

What can be seen beyond the possibility of deception is a general lack of understanding as to how to approach the issue of potential deception. How can we ensure deception is avoided? In this book, I will point out the Scriptural test. This is a Scripture that I rarely hear being discussed, and later I will discuss Bible verses that talk about protecting us from deception and the common theme that runs through them.

1 John 4:1 Beloved, do not believe every spirit [speaking through a self-proclaimed prophet]; instead, test the spirits to see whether

they are from God because many false prophets and teachers have gone out into the world AMP

I explain this verse in more detail in chapter 14:8.

3.2 Deception and the Demonic realm

2 Corinthians 4:4 Among them the god of this world [Satan] has blinded the minds of the unbelieving to prevent them from seeing the illuminating light of the gospel of the glory of Christ, who is the image of God. AMP

Ephesians 2:2 in which you once walked. You were following the ways of this world [influenced by this present age], in accordance with the prince of the power of the air (Satan), the spirit who is now at work in the disobedient [the unbelieving, who fight against the purposes of God] AMP

2 Corinthians 11:14also warns believers that workers of Satan appear as servants of righteousness

2 Corinthians 11:14 And no wonder, since Satan himself masquerades as an angel of light. 15 So it is no great surprise if his servants also masquerade as servants of righteousness, but their end will correspond with their deeds. AMP

Our enemy Satan seeks to deceive the elect and there are multiple verses that warn us that we have a spiritual enemy who seeks to deceive people. The question becomes how should we respond when we are aware that we face such opposition. The first thing is to be humble and pray that God keeps us all free from such deception. Then we need to adopt biblical standards in order to discern when deception is present and how to avoid it.

The next section presents a range of verses that expose the problem of false knowledge.

3.3 There is a Clear Link between False Knowledge and Deception.

In 1 Corinthians 1:20, there is a clear statement that the wisdom of the world is foolishness to God. There are also references to Greek thinking in the words philosopher, orator and logician. These words are all associated with Greek thinking. Greece is the birthplace of philosophy and home to Aristotle, Socrates and Plato, to name but a few. Oratory persuasion or rhetoric also began in Ancient Greece in a school of Greek philosophers known as Sophists around 600BC. The famous Greek philosopher Aristotle wrote a book called *Rhetoric* in the 4th century BC. The idea of logic also started in Ancient Greece with Aristotle and his syllogisms which are the foundations of deductive logic. (13)

There is another reference to the deception involved in Greek thinking and Gnosticism in 1 Timothy 4:1-4. (A more detailed discussion of Greek thinking is given in Chapter 6)

1 Timothy 4:1 But the [Holy] Spirit explicitly and unmistakably declares that in later times some will turn away from the faith, paying attention instead to deceitful and seductive spirits and doctrines of demons, 2 [misled] by the hypocrisy of liars whose consciences are seared as with a branding iron [leaving them incapable of ethical functioning], 3 who forbid marriage and advocate

abstaining from [certain kinds of] foods which God has created to be gratefully shared by those who believe and have [a clear] knowledge of the truth. 4 For everything God has created is good, and nothing is to be rejected if it is received with gratitude. AMP.

Gnosticism has been previously mentioned. Gnosticism includes a dualism that says the intellectual world is pure yet the material world is evil. The idea that priests should not marry, and religious people should be kept separated from the world in monasteries comes from Gnosticism.

Isaiah 47:10 refers to Satanic power and his verse explains what has led Satan astray. The answer is wisdom and knowledge.

Isaiah 47:10 "For you [Babylon] have trusted and felt confident in your wickedness; you have said, 'No one sees me.' Your wisdom and your knowledge have led you astray, And you have said in your heart (mind), 'I am, and there is no one besides me AMP

In Isaiah 44:20 the idolater is led astray by a deceived mind.

Isaiah: 44:20 That kind of man (the idolater) feeds on ashes [and is satisfied with ashes]! A deceived mind has led him astray, so that he cannot save himself, or ask, "Is this thing [that I am holding] in my right hand, not a lie?AMP.

Yet conversely, we are assured that in Christ all the treasures of wisdom and knowledge are hidden. in Colossians 2:2

Colossians 2:2 [For my hope is] that their hearts may be encouraged as they are knit together in [unselfish] love, so that they may have all the riches that come from the full assurance of understanding [the joy of salvation], resulting in a true [and more intimate] knowledge of the mystery of God, that is, Christ, 3 in whom are hidden all the treasures of wisdom and knowledge [regarding the word and purposes of God].

3.4 The Holy Spirit is the Solution to Deception.

2 Timothy 1:14 Guard [with the greatest care] and keep unchanged, the treasure [that precious truth] which has been entrusted to you [that is, the good news about salvation through personal faith in Christ Jesus], through [the help of] the Holy Spirit who dwells in us. AMP.

John 16:13 However, when He, the Spirit of truth, has come, He will guide you into all truth; for He will not speak on His own *authority,* but whatever He hears He will speak; and He will tell you things to come. NKJV

1 John 2:27 speaks about the anointing which is the presence of the Holy Spirit in us, and how it teaches us all things.

1 John 2:27 As for you, the anointing [the special gift, the preparation] which you received from Him remains [permanently] in you, and you have no need for anyone to teach you. But just as His anointing teaches you [giving you insight through the presence of the Holy Spirit] about all things, and is true and is not a lie, and just as His anointing has taught you, you must remain in Him [being rooted in Him, knit to Him]. AMP

3.5 The 1 John example of serious Deception

1 John 2:18 Children, it is the last hour [the end of this age]; and just as you heard that the antichrist is coming [the one who will oppose Christ and attempt to replace Him], even now many antichrists (false teachers) have appeared, which confirms our belief that it is the last hour.

1 John 2:19 They went out from us [seeming at first to be Christians], but they were not really of us [because they were not truly born again and spiritually transformed]; for if they had been of us, they would have remained with us; but they went out [teaching false doctrine] so that it would be clearly shown that none of them are of us. AMP

The deception was caused by a group of people who initially belonged to the church and were thought to be genuine disciples, but it was eventually understood they were teaching a false doctrine. Given that this was described as a teaching issue, it would be reasonable to assume that this teaching issue would be detected by study and academic rigour. There must have been a discrepancy between what they taught and Scriptural values. Contrary to this assumption, the problem was not detected intellectually.

There are a number of important points that John makes about discerning this false doctrine:-

First: The deceived ones were within the church. This means they were not against claiming to be Christian even though they believed in a false doctrine.

Second: They had come under the influence of the spirits of antichrist.

Third: The key factor that separated these false believers and the true ones was the anointing of the Holy One or, in the words of the KJV version, the unction from the Holy One.

1 John 2:20 But you have an anointing from the Holy One [you have been set apart, specially gifted and prepared by the Holy Spirit], and all of you know [the truth because He teaches us, illuminates our minds, and guards us from error]. AMP

1 John 2:20 But ye have an unction from the Holy One, and ye know all things. KJV

The key to avoiding this deception was the presence of the Holy Spirit and, as we read before according to the Amplified version of 1 John 2:1:9 those under this deception were "not truly born again and spiritually transformed". The fundamental problem was spiritual. In addition, the solution was the revelation that came from being spiritual or, in biblical terms, having an anointing. In the verses listed below, we can see more confirmation for the general principles that are being outlined in this chapter i.e. the root cause of deception is spiritual and the Holy Spirit is critical in the process of detecting deception.

Other questions that can be further analysed are "what is the true nature of this deception?" or more precisely "what is the nature of the spirit of the antichrist?" The traditional understanding is that it is something similar to atheism or antagonism to Christianity. I don't think this view bears scrutiny. The reason is that these people were within the church and it is hard to understand a scenario where any atheist would either want to be in a church, or appear to be a true believer. The question then becomes, "what sort of deception were they involved in?"

The basic facts of the 1 John situation are confirmed even by conservative evangelical (non-charismatic) scholarship. Even one of the most strident anti-charismatic authors, John MacArthur has written, " Most likely, John was combating the beginnings of this virulent heresy that threatened to destroy the fundamentals of the faith and the churches. Gnosticism, influenced by such philosophers as Plato, advocated a dualism asserting that matter was inherently evil and spirit was inherently good. As a result of this presupposition, these false teachers, although attributing some form of deity to Christ, denied his true humanity to preserve him from evil. It also claimed elevated knowledge, a higher truth known only to those in on the deep things. Only the initiated had the mystical knowledge of the truth that was higher even than the Scripture." (14) What we are reading here is MacArthur's argument that Gnostics were able to present themselves as Christians and yet denied that Jesus was human. This will be discussed more shortly when we look at 1 John 4:1-3.

The central tenet of Evangelicalism is that it is "Bible-believing", yet typically Evangelicalism does not embrace the contemporary gifts of the Spirit. The *1, 2, & 3 John: Evangelical Exegetical Commentary* by Gary W. Derickson confirms the historical context of these books. When introducing 1 John 2, Derickson recognises this group of people are a precursor to Gnosticism and he labels this belief system as proto-Gnosticism. (15) According to Derickson St. John anticipated Gnosticism's development and the threat that it was to become to the church. In identifying this problem, John was warning the church and seeking to reduce Gnosticism's potential to damage the influence of the gospel message. In hindsight, the way John targets Gnosticism specifically and Greek thinking, in general, shows a level of prophetic insight that could be expected from the author of the book of Revelation. It is no accident that John targeted Gnosticism. (16)

An early form of Gnosticism was Doceticism which believed that Jesus only appeared to have a physical body. This meant Jesus was considered to be only a spirit and actually didn't die on the cross. It only appeared that this happened. MacArthur correctly states "Such heretical views destroy not only the true humanity of Jesus, but also the atonement, for Jesus must not only have been truly God, but also the truly human (and physically real) man who actually suffered and died upon the cross, in order to be the acceptable substitutionary sacrifice for sin (cf. Heb. 2:14–17). The biblical view of Jesus affirms his complete humanity as well as his full deity" (17)

While Gnosticism has many variations and is difficult to precisely define, it has two core beliefs. Both of these beliefs have their roots in Platonic philosophy. The first belief is the Gnostic concept that secret knowledge was the key to salvation. This concept is in line with general Greek thinking focus on intellectualism (discussed in Chapter 6). The second belief is derived from the dualism of Greek thought. This dualistic perspective separates matter and spirit. Physical matter is considered to be evil and the spirit is considered good. This dualistic premise leads to several heretical ideas. God is a pure spirit and Doceticism believes He could not create a material universe because there is evil inherent in the material realm. Some forms of Gnosticism talk about a demiurge, or lesser God, who was responsible for creation. (18)

Another belief within Doceticism is that Jesus could not have come as a man in the flesh because he was too spiritual and Holy to be a material being. This belief is very specifically addressed in 1 John 4:1-3 where we read about the importance of recognising that Jesus came in the flesh. Here John is writing in a very pointed way, and rejecting the influence of Gnosticism, especially this early form of Docetism.

1 Beloved, do not believe every spirit, but test the spirits, whether they are of God; because many false prophets have gone out into the world. 2 By this you know the Spirit of God: Every spirit that confesses that Jesus Christ has come in the flesh is of God, 3 and every spirit that does not confess that Jesus Christ has come in the flesh is not of God. And this is the spirit of the Antichrist, which you have heard was coming and is now already in the world. NKJV

This verse presents a number of key points. First, the idea that Jesus came in the flesh is critical to our faith. The concept of a saviour dying for us makes no sense unless he was human. The whole concept of covenant requires Jesus to be human. This test of confessing that Jesus came in the flesh is very important. This test enables us to determine whether a spirit or a prophet, is from God or not. Knowing if they are from God by observing their fruit is a less precise test. This is a significant test to help us determine what is really from God, yet in my experience, it is rarely referenced. This points to the fact its significance and meaning are not fully comprehended in the broader church.

3.6 An overview of Deception

In 1 John 2, we can see there was deception in the early church that was undetected for some time. This pattern is seen again in 1 John 4.1 which warns believers about deception in the church.

In 1 John 2, the source of that deception was the spirit of antichrist. This deception had demonic origins. In 4.2 we saw the link between deception and the demonic realm.

In 1 John 2:21 & 22, we see lies coming from the spirit of antichrist. This is in line with 4.3 where we see a clear link with false knowledge.

In 1 John 2:19, we see it is specifically the anointing and not academic knowledge that reveals deception.

In summary, 1 John 2 teaches that the Holy Spirit is central in unveiling deception. In this situation, we very specifically see the anointing teaching and protecting the people of God from deception.

These findings point to a biblical pattern.

We should expect that deception exists.

We should expect the source of that deception to be demonic.

We see that false teaching is connected to deception.

We see that the way to discern deception is spiritual or via anointing.

There is a clear priority that the church needs to be spiritual in order to avoid deception.

3.7 Additional Information on Deception

The idea is that because the body is evil material it should be treated harshly. Practices like self-flagellation come from this idea.

Because the body is evil we should expect it to sin and we should allow such practices and not be concerned. Some even denied the existence of sin (1 John 1:8–10 (19)

For some mankind is too sinful to have the Holy Spirit within us, but this is clearly a contradiction of the Scriptures including 1 John 4:4.

Chapter Four

The Modern Church and Scripture

The idea that deception exists within many of today's expressions of Christianity is part of the thesis of this book. As uncomfortable as that may make some readers feel, it should be understood that this idea is shared by some leading thinkers within the church.

First, we have the words of Charles Spurgeon who was arguably the faith's greatest preacher of the 1800s. Spurgeon said, "he could find ten men who would die for the Bible for everyone who would read it!" (20) Spurgeon's point is that many people who describe themselves as committed Christians have a limited understanding of the Bible. This lack of biblical understanding is further underlined by the fact that there is a very respected journal for evangelical leaders which was found to have less than 1 per cent of its content covering even a single scriptural reference. (21)

A more considered analysis has been undertaken by N.T Wright who is a respected conservative evangelical theologian and academic. As a theologian, he has held professorships at Oxford and as a churchman, he has been an Anglican Bishop. In his January series of lectures at Calvin College in 2012, (22) N.T Wright discusses the way the church of the western world has developed a distorted idea of God. Wright argues that the main source of this problem is something that many have seen as foundational to our faith. Wright believes the problem goes way back to the creeds, specifically in the way the creeds have placed their emphasis on the birth and death of Jesus. These creeds are strangely silent about what happens between them. In addition, these creeds are thought to embrace the theology of Paul, yet, as we will see in chapter 14, there are aspects of Paul's writing that the creeds avoid.

For Wright, this creedal presentation of God is very similar to being a Deist description. These descriptions describe a distant God who is hard to understand and in Wright's words "reaches in from time to time and stirs the pot from the outside producing what we then call miraculous events with no natural cause". (23) Wright then challenges the view of those who believe that Jesus died on the cross and his only focus was so that we can go to heaven. For Wright, this description is fundamentally unbiblical. Wright argues that the gospels proclaim that Jesus died as King of the Jews. In doing this, He triumphantly overcomes the powers of the world. These are ideas that "cannot be captured by our usual atonement theology formula" (24) Wright is not denying that Jesus came to save us, but beyond atonement theology, there are "signposts to that larger almost inexpressible reality of new covenant and new creation " (25)

Wright argues our salvation is not for our sake alone and that "the kingdom of God is not just part of God's plan so we can have a nice time. Salvation is part of God's kingdom plan. We have been purchased by his blood not for just for our sake but so that we can become a royal priesthood and reign on earth as it says in Revelation 5:10." (26)

Revelation 10:26 And have made us kings and priests to our God, And we shall reign on the earth." (NKJV)

Wright argues that the church has adopted an incorrect understanding of the distant nature of God and that the church has a superficial understanding of the nature of God's kingdom. Wright summarises by saying, "You cannot read the gospels just for information," (27) instead of invoking the Living Lord, we are in a church that has " forgotten what the gospels are all about". (28)

The core problem, from Wright's perspective, is that the church has become comfortable with a Deist and distant view of our Heavenly Father. As will be explained later, all these problems are consistent with the church adopting Greek thinking and interpreting Scripture through that thinking. N.T. Wright provides evidence of serious evangelical scholarship that recognises the disconnect between Scriptural values and current church practice. Wright argues there must be change and the problem is serious. (29) N.T Wright may have developed conclusions that are contrary to the way our contemporary church culture thinks, however, if we start with an accurate and literal interpretation of Scripture, these conclusions are difficult to repudiate. This book argues that not only are Wright's statements absolutely biblical, but in addition, they point to another truth. This is the truth that our churches have often focused on a natural and Deist interpretation of Scripture. Many parts of our modern church studiously avoid any discussion of miracles. This approach makes overt expressions of spirituality unwelcome. This is a process that has been heavily influenced by the European enlightenment. It has been described as the secularisation of the church.

Charles Taylor discusses this concept of secularisation in his book *A Secular Age* (2007), Taylor argues against the subtraction theory' of secularisation. (30) He defines this as the process where religion loses the imagination of the people and replaces it with science and rationality. He sees this process of secularisation as dominating Western Christianity. One commentator on Taylor is Tom Frame who interprets Taylor's view this way: The Christian desire to improve humanity evolved into a form of humanism when it is seen through the lens of the European Enlightenment. Its aspirations were almost exclusively temporal. This view points to secularisation as not being defined by the lack of churches as much as the lack of spirituality within those churches. (31) With Frame's understanding of Taylor, we get a view that very much aligns with that of N.T.Wright. Each of these thinkers is pointing to this lack of spirituality.

In the coming chapters, this book looks at the history of the church. The church has moved from the spirituality of Jesus and Paul in the first century to a church that has become to be dominated by Greek thinking. Along the way, much has been lost. Later there is a proposal to return the church to true spirituality and a kingdom mentality.

Chapter Five

Greek and Hebrew Thought compared

I t is the thesis of this book that Greek thinking has come to dominate the church yet the best way to understand the Bible is through Hebrew thinking. This chapter provides a brief introduction to the differences between these two modes of thought. It should be understood that today's Western education system is based on Greek thinking. Most people with a modern education have been taught to think from this Greek perspective. It all begins at a young age. The Greek thinking approach to knowing God is to seek knowledge about God. Alternatively, the Hebrew mind says we should know God himself. The logical extension of the Greek approach is to build libraries of books like systematic theologies and listen to sermons that enable us to develop our understanding of God. The ultimate goal is to understand his attributes. Alternatively, the Hebrew approach encourages people to fall to their knees and seek the person of God directly. (32)

The Greek approach encourages us to read multiple Bible commentaries and books containing the wisdom of scholars. The Hebrew approach encourages people to read the Bible by themselves and seek the Spirit of God for personal revelation. (33)

In his book, *How the Church Lost the Way and How It Can Find It Again,* Steve Maltz (34) helps us to further understand the problem. Greek thinking seeks to develop concepts and ideas that explain the world. If we look at the range of literature on systematic theology, we can see many principles that the writer believes will help us understand God. The overriding approach of Greek thinking is developing our capacity to think about God. Humans are seen as the ultimate decision-makers who are capable of interpreting the world around us. Alternatively, the Hebrew approach is the search for revelation. The Hebrew mind approaches God as the source of this revelation. The Hebrew mind approaches God on the basis that we are limited and fallible. Humanity seeks to understand God's wisdom, and the first step to approaching that wisdom is to acknowledge that God's wisdom is superior to ours. (35)

Scriptures that express this idea include:

Isaiah 40:28 Have you not known? Have you not heard? The everlasting God, the Lord, The Creator of the ends of the earth, Neither faints nor is weary. His understanding is unsearchable. NKJV

Isaiah 55:8 "For My thoughts *are* not your thoughts, Nor *are* your ways My ways," says the Lord.9 "For *as* the heavens are higher than the earth, So are My ways higher than your ways, And My thoughts than your thoughts. NKJV.

John 1:1-3 1 In the beginning was the Word, and the Word was with God, and the Word was God. 2 He was in the beginning with God. 3 All things were made through Him, and without Him, nothing was made that was made. NKJV.

There are however significant differences between Greek and Hebrew thinking. An example of these differences is that there is no word in Hebrew that means Mind. In the English Old Testament, the original Hebrew words translated into mind include heart, soul and spirit. (37) The reason is these are the spiritual places in man where we listen to the mind of our Heavenly Father. But this is a completely different understanding from the English and Greek language understandings. Steve Maltz has an account in his book *How the Church Lost the Truth: And How it Can Find it Again,* In it he recounts how he was browsing through a 2016 Christian theology book which has been described as, one of the most widely used textbooks in the world of Christian Theology. (38) The author is a respected theologian, however, Maltz was struck by two things:

First, the detailed index didn't have a single reference that included the terms, Jewish, Israel or Hebrew (or Hebraic).

Second, this text stated that the key debates in the early Church relating to Jesus were conducted in Greek and were viewed through the presuppositions of Greek philosophy. It would seem according to the worlds of Theology and Christian history, the faith that was once defined as Jewish-based has become a Greek philosophy, one that is defined by the thoughts of Socrates, Plato and their like. While this analysis may be a simplistic deduction, often simple observations can reveal a deeper truth, in this case, one that the church seems to rarely discuss. Maltz then observed, that in this same book index, Plato had the same number of references as St.Paul, while Aristotle had more than double that number and Moses had zero. (39)

Chapter Six

Greek Thinking

The Greek philosopher Protagoras (481-411 BC) said "Man is the measure of all things of what is and what is not." (40) This philosophy provided the foundation for Hellenism which was devoted to the supremacy of human beings and human accomplishment. The cultural tradition of the Greeks is Hellenism and this was the prevalent worldview immediately preceding the birth of Jesus and during the time of early Christianity. Socrates was born in Athens (c.469 BC -399 BC). While there were influential Greek thinkers like Pythagoras that came before him, the ideas of Socrates are considered to be foundational to Western philosophy. It is widely thought that Socrates was one of the wisest men in history. While pre-Socratic philosophers focused on the natural world, Socrates emphasised human experience and concepts of individual morality and living. He also examined broader issues of society and politics. Socrates never committed any of his thoughts to writing and our current knowledge of him is entirely based on the writings of his students and contemporaries which includes Plato among others. Unfortunately, those writings are not always factual or consistent. Most people know Socrates because of his Socratic method. The Socratic method continually asks questions in a way that is designed to expose the contradictions of a student's thoughts and then guides the student to think through the issues. This enables students to come to a conclusion that better fits the facts. Plato was born in Athens c. 428 BC to 347 BC and his parents were members of the Greek aristocracy. Plato's upbringing provided him with an education from many distinguished teachers. It was, however, Socrates and his ability to debate and create a dialogue that had the greatest impact on Plato. This influence can be seen in the way that much of today's knowledge about Socrates comes from the writings of Plato. Despite being expected by his family to enter the world of politics, Plato studied philosophy and began writing and travelling. Plato studied under Pythagoras in Sicily. When he returned to Athens he founded the Academy. This was a school where he and others taught philosophy and mathematics. This Academy became the model for the universities of today. "Academy" was the actual name of his house. The academy was open to the public, yet most of the participants were upper-class men. It did not, at least during Plato's time, charge fees for membership. The academy was not in Plato's time a "school" as there was no clear distinction between teachers and students, or even a formal curriculum. In Plato's time, there was not any specific doctrine to teach. (41)(42)(43)

Plato is best known for his teaching about the Theory of Forms or Ideas. In this teaching Forms and Ideas have identical meanings. When the words Form and Idea are spelt with a capital letter it highlights they are being used in the Platonic sense. Socrates believed when he asked the question "What is beauty?" or "What is courage?", he wasn't searching for a definition but rather he was seeking to discover the nature of some abstract entity that had an actual existence. According to Socrates, these entities did not exist in a specific time and place but had a kind of universal existence that was independent of a specific place and time. In our world, we can observe beautiful places and objects as well as specific acts that encompass elements like courage or compassion. These actions are performed by individual people and are always fleeting, yet they may partake of the timeless essence of true courage or true compassion. These ideals are indestructible and exist on their own. Plato took these principles as they relate to the nature of morals and values and wrote that they apply to all of reality. This means that, according to Plato, everything that exists in this present world is an ephemeral, decaying copy of the ideal form. Plato argues that these ideals and forms have a permanent and indestructible existence beyond the material limits of space and time.

Aristotle (384-322 BC) was born in the city of Stagira. His father died when he was still young which meant he had a guardian in his younger life who sent him to Athens at about 17 so he could be educated at Plato's Academy. Aristotle stayed at the Academy for about 20 years. Later, around 335 BC, he founded a school called the Lyceum in Athens. He died at the age of 62. Aristotle acknowledged Plato's genius and recognised his indebtedness to him, however, his philosophy was fundamentally different to Plato's. Aristotle eventually became a tutor to Alexander the Great.

Plotinus (204-269)AD was born in 204 and died in 269 AD. Plotinus was an Egyptian with a Roman name. He wrote in Greek, and some describe him as the last of the great Greek philosophers. Plotinus can also be considered to be antiquity's last great philosopher. Plotinus developed a mystical emphasis on the writings of Plato and came to be known as a Neo-Platonist. He never mentioned Christianity in his writings, and he cannot be considered to be a Christian. (44) Despite this, his philosophy strongly influenced two of the most influential Christian thinkers before the European Enlightenment. They were St. Augustine and St. Thomas Aquinas. Plotinus played a significant role in the development of Christian thought. (45) Dean Inge a famous 20th-century Christian writer, describes Plotinus as "the great thinker who must be, for all time, the classical representative of mystical philosophy. No other mystical thinker even approaches Plotinus in power and insight and profound spiritual penetration." (46)

The emergence of Gnosticism, which became a popular heresy in the early church, came out of thoughts based on the Platonic worldview. It is difficult to give Gnosticism a precise definition as it includes many groups, with their individual variations, all coming under the same Gnostic umbrella. There are, however, key ideas that define Gnosticism. First, Gnosticism is based on the Greek word Gnosis which means knowledge. The Gnostics believe that the key to salvation is secret knowledge. Second, Gnosticism comes with a fundamentally dualistic framework. The world of ideas is ideal and is viewed positively, whereas the world of the body and the material realm is seen as evil. (47) Historically, the main recent opponent of Hellenism and Greek thinking has been Alfred Harnack (1851-1930) Harnack, later known as von Harnack, a German theologian who sought to reject the influence of Hellenism within the church. According to Harnack, Hellenism was "the spirit of Greek philosophy at work on the soil of the gospel" (48)

6.1 Introduction to Greek thought.

Hellenism was based on the belief that human beings are the ultimate source of truth and authority in the universe. Since then, human beings were considered the "measure of all," and human wisdom was deemed to be the greatest wisdom. What could not be understood or explained was thought of as false. Human accomplishments in athletics, the arts, and architecture became the motivating drive of society. The human body was considered the ultimate in beauty so nudity, in art, in the baths, and in sports, was common. The accumulation of material possessions in order to provide oneself with luxury and comfort was a common pursuit. What could be more natural than to get the most out of life? After all, life's greatest goal was to be the best at any pursuit. (49)

The Hellenists tried to build their society on their gods who were human creations. In effect, they worshipped themselves. Because they had nothing greater than themselves on which to base their worldview and society, their society eventually collapsed. No society can exist for a long time when it creates its own view of truth.

Was Hellenism, at its roots, really new? No. The first evidence of it is recorded when Satan asked Eve, "Did God really say"? (Gen. 3:1). Eve, and then Adam faced an earth-shaking choice: the need to choose the ultimate source of truth in the universe. When Adam and Eve decided to disobey God's command not to eat from the tree (Gen. 2:16-17), they decided for themselves what was right and best for them. They effectively sought independence from God and crowned themselves as the ultimate authority in the universe. (50)

In contrast, the worldview of Christianity is based on God as the ultimate truth and authority. His revelation is the source of our vision for how we live and the priorities we make. The resulting values are absolute, not merely creations of our imaginations. The belief in the dignity of each person comes from our understanding that we are created in God's image. In a Christian worldview sees God is the ultimate authority in the universe. Life is to be lived for Him and not for us. The ultimate beauty comes from God, not humankind. Truth is what God has revealed and it is up to his people to discover it. (51)

The core beliefs of Greek thinking or Hellenism define the priorities of today's culture. Today's version of Hellenism is Humanism which promotes the idea that human beings are the ultimate authority in the universe. The humanist perspective defines truth according to what the human mind can discover, demonstrate, and understand. It glorifies the achievements of humanity and is driven to be number one, yet there is also an obsession with comfort and pleasure. The love of pleasure brings with it a focus on sexuality, as well as a lack of compassion for other people. It brings a democratic perspective. All of these ideas were included in the belief systems of the ancient Greek philosophers.

Today we commonly hear phrases like: "Just do it." "If it feels good, go with it." "I can do whatever I want with my body." Our public education system is full of these, and other, sayings which are based on Greek thought. Truth is defined by what each person can logically understand and demonstrate. As a consequence, our society has embraced a system of values that are very similar to those in the Greek world, around the time of the early church. (52)

The Greek mindset is based on the thinking of the Greek Philosophers. First, this chapter provides an overview of the most influential Greek philosophers. Influential is defined as those that have influenced the church and its thinking, rather than a general cultural influence. This is followed by an examination of how this Greek thinking has influenced the church fathers. It will be shown that there has been a historical process which has meant that the church of today has largely chosen Greek thought over Hebrew thought. The significance of this will be discussed later. (53)

6.2 Socrates

"The unexamined life is not worth living," is a quote often attributed to Socrates. Socrates believed that the ability to understand oneself was an essential element of wisdom and that actions were related to an individual's intelligence. This approach was part of Socrates' unique way of understanding knowledge, consciousness, and morality. These ideas of Socrates changed philosophy forever. (54)

6.3 The Socratic Method

Part of the Socratic method is the elenchus, which is a method which refutes the claims of a student in 4 key steps.

A student makes a statement to Socrates. Socrates then refutes this statement or asks a follow-up question like "What is courage?"

Once the student answers the question, Socrates would seek to present a scenario which highlights the inadequacy or possible falsity of the original answer. Following on from our previous example, the student might give "endurance of the soul, " as their definition of courage. Socrates could challenge this definition by saying "Courage is a fine thing," yet "Ignorant endurance is not a fine thing."

The student would agree to this and Socrates would provide a revised definition that addresses the issues raised after their original proposition is made. Socrates proves that the student's original statement was false and that the revised definition is in fact true. The student answers again and Socrates continues the process of refuting and refining the student's answers until they get closer to the actual truth.

The Socratic Method is still widely used in law schools throughout the western world. Students are asked to summarise a judge's argument and whether they agree with the argument or not. The professor then asks a series of questions that challenge the student to defend his answer. The Socratic Method is used so that students learn to think critically and develop answers based on logic and reason. This challenge includes the ability to cope with the issues and anomalies presented by the professor. (55)

6.4 Plato

Plato was born in Athens c. 428 BC to 347 BC and his parents were members of the Greek aristocracy. Plato's upbringing provided him with an education from many distinguished teachers. It was, however, Socrates and his ability to debate and create a dialogue that had the greatest impact on Plato. This influence can be seen in the way that much of today's knowledge about Socrates comes from the writings of Plato. Despite being expected by his family to enter the world of politics, Plato studied philosophy and began writing and travelling. Plato studied under Pythagoras in Sicily. When he returned to Athens he founded the Academy. This was a school where he and others taught philosophy and mathematics. This Academy became the model for the universities of today. "Academy" was the actual name of his house. The academy was open to the public, yet most of the participants were upper-class men. It did not, at least during Plato's time, charge fees for membership. The academy was not in Plato's time a "school" as there was no clear distinction between teachers and students, or even a formal curriculum. In Plato's time, there was not any specific doctrine to teach. (56)(57)(58)

6.5 Plato's Theory of Forms or Ideas.

Plato argued that his belief in Forms was supported by different arguments. One argument was based on the study of physics. For Plato, the more he studied physics, the more he was convinced that there were mathematical relationships behind all the forces he observed in the material world. These Forms revealed an underlying order and harmony while the surface of our everyday world can seem so chaotic. Plato's dualistic view is that our eyes and senses discern this chaos, yet only the trained mind and intellect have the capacity to see this overriding harmony and perfection. In our visible world, as we understand it through our senses, nothing lasts and nothing stays the same. This is how Plato sought to express the nature of our material reality. As Plato liked to put it, "everything in this world is always becoming something else, but nothing ever just permanently is". (59)

According to Platonic thought, the world is separated into a physical world that is understood through the senses and a higher reality that is understood intellectually. This dualism has been extremely influential in the world of Christianity. As the early Christian Church separated itself from the synagogue, the leaders came from educated male members. Most of these were educated in the Greek academies which promoted this Greek worldview. (60) There are great similarities between the Greek worldview and a Christian worldview, The Platonic idea is that the perfect is discovered by the intellect and our senses teach us about the material world which is destined to decay. The Christian view is all Godly truth is understood spiritually. In addition, while humanity lives in a fallen world, God has declared his creation as good.

6.6 Aristotle

The two most influential Greek philosophers were Plato and Aristotle.

Plato and Aristotle represent two alternative approaches to philosophy. The Platonic approach places only a limited value on knowledge of the world as understood by our senses. For Plato and philosophers like him, the ultimate focus is something that lies beyond the obvious. Alternatively, Aristotle represents philosophers who believe that this world should be the object of philosophy. Plato paved the way for the rationalist philosophers especially, in the 17th and 18th centuries. Plato believed that knowledge coming from our sensory experience often deceives us. Aristotle alternatively provided the inspiration for the writings of the great empiricist philosophers, also from the 17th and 18th centuries. They believe that reliable information requires direct examination and observation. The tension between the perspectives of Plato and Aristotle continues today. Christians tend to be more attracted to Plato's approach, yet the scientific approach of modern culture tends to prefer the thinking of Aristotle.

Aristotle's thinking covered a diverse range of studies included: rhetoric, logic, physics, psychology, political science, economics, metaphysics, meteorology and ethics. For a single man, his achievements are simply stunning. In addition, Aristotle coined technical terms that survive until today. They include energy, dynamic, induction, demonstration, substance, attribute, essence, property, accident, category, topic, proposition, and universal. On top of all this, he systematised logic by working out which forms of inference were valid and which were invalid. In other words, Aristotle has studied what can be logically said from a proposition and what cannot be said, even if it seems possible. Aristotle gave all these different forms of inference names. For two thousand years, the study of logic meant the study of Aristotle's logic. (61)62(63)

6.7 Plotinus the Neo-Platonist.

Plotinus argued that Platonic philosophy was central to the intellectual development of Christianity. Plotinus and Plato both had a significant influence on the development of early Christian thought. Plotinus taught that, since ultimate reality consists of Plato's Ideal Forms, what exists is ultimately mental and therefore, for something to be created is for it to be thought. There are, he believed, three ascending levels of a human soul. The lowest part of the soul is the human appetite. The next level up is the part of the soul that apprehends the Ideal Forms, which is the intellect. The highest level is described as the good, where reflective human beings attempt to ascend towards oneness with the good. Christian thinkers seeking to embrace Platonism have interpreted this as human beings aspiring to oneness with God in a world that has been created by the mind of God. (64)

Neo-Platonism is a highly abstract philosophy that stresses the infinite beyondness of what they describe as the divine source and origin of all things. Neo-Platonism argues that God's existence is so transcendent and incomprehensible that there are no concepts in Neo-Platonism for either a personal God or for a purposeful creation out of nothing. (60)

6.8 Gnosticism

As we have read one of the key themes of the epistle of 1 John, especially chapter 4, is the humanity of Jesus. This text argues against the Gnostic idea that a physical body is too evil for Jesus to live in.

1 John 4:1 Beloved, do not believe every spirit [speaking through a self-proclaimed prophet]; instead, test the spirits to see whether they are from God because many false prophets and teachers have gone out into the world. 2 By this you know and recognize the Spirit of God: every spirit that acknowledges and confesses [the fact] that Jesus Christ has [actually] come in the flesh [as a man] is from God [God is its source]; v3 and every spirit that does not confess Jesus [acknowledging that He has come in the flesh, but would deny any of the Son's true nature] is not of God; this is the spirit of the antichrist, which you have heard is coming and is now already in the world. AMP.

6.9 Harnack and Greek Thought

Harnack argued that Hellenization (Hellenization being the American form of the word Hellenism, both describe the Greek influence on society) was behind the intellectualisation of Christianity through Greek philosophy. According to Harnack, this intellectualisation has led Christianity to become an institutional faith with a diminished personal experience of the Gospel. Harnack wrote that Christianity was a living faith that had been reduced to an expression of orthodox dogma and statements that require our personal assent. Harnack rejected the intellectualisation of Christianity and the way it became defined as an academic doctrine. (65)

In the introduction, we learned the basic differences between Greek and Hebrew thought. Greek thought is an academic approach where people analyse things critically from a distance. Alternatively, Hebrew thought is seeking to relate to what God is saying in an intimate and personal way. Harnack saw Christianity as a living faith and rejected the view that it was an expression of orthodox dogma. Harnack sought an acceptance of Hebrew thought and encouraged the rejection of Greek thought. (66)

Chapter Seven

The History of Greek Influence and Hellenization

This book looks at the difference between Greek and Hebrew thinking as well as the impact that Greek thinking has had on the way we understand the Bible. Hellenization influenced more than just the early church. Hellenization was a significant influence on the development of the Jewish people. One of the early reasons that Greek thinking influenced the church to the degree it did was the Hellenization of the Jewish community. This understanding of the way Hellenization influenced the Jewish people has increased since the release of Martin Hengel's 1974 book *Judaism and Hellenism*. (67) (Again, Hellenization is an American term, and Hellenism a UK term, both are essentially interchangeable). The process of Hellenization had already made a profound impact on the Jewish faith prior to the arrival of Jesus. This opened the door for Hellenization to influence the church.

The very early Christians were mostly Jewish and Jesus was under-stood from the perspective of Judaism. These believers understood that Jesus of Nazareth was the long-awaited Jewish Messiah and he was destined to fulfil many prophecies as well as lay the foun-dations for the Kingdom of God. The definition of the kingdom of God was, as we read before, a matter of some debate. Most early Christians understood Jesus was bringing new dimensions of faith and probably were thinking in terms of the completion of Ju-daism. Jesus certainly set that in place, but not in the way that was expected (68). Eventually, Christians came to distinguish them-selves from Jews, and Jews would begin to distinguish themselves from Christians. The early second century saw this distinction becoming more defined. Of the twelve apostles, only Luke came from a non-Jewish background. As the second century continued Christians faced persecution from multiple sources: the Romans, Jews and pagans. The Collective effect of this persecution meant that beyond 100AD the influence of the apostles was as good as gone. Ominously, the few replacements that were available were educated in the dominant Greek culture of the day. They brought with them the Greek language and thinking of the day. The Greek Education System and the Spread of Hellenism dominated Gentile society at the time of Jesus. While Greece was not the political power that it was in the time of Alexander the Great, it had de-veloped literary supremacy. During the Christian era, Rome ruled Greece, however, Greece dominated the world of literature and this influence spread across the Gentile world. The first step in the transition between Greek and Hebrew thinking was Philo's idea that God tends to be unknowable. Contrary to this, Jesus taught that it is possible to know God and John 14:6-7 and John 16:2-3 both record him confirming the Hebrew understanding.

7.1 Hellenization of Judaism

Hellenization began with the adoption of the Greek language which opened the door to Greek philosophy and ideals. This understanding of Hellenization began with J. G. Droysen (1808-1884), a German historian. Droysen wrote about Hellenism and the Jewish faith (69). According to Droysen, Hellenism began with Alexander the Great (70). Around the time of Alexander the Great (356-323 BC), Greek culture, which was spread by both the Macedonians and the Romans, invaded the empires and cultures of the time. These included Persia, Egypt, Syria, India and Palestine (71). The influence of Hellenization/Hellenism is specifically mentioned in Acts 6:1 of the Amplified version of the Bible. In this verse, we find the word Hellenists. The word Hellenist describes a Greek-speaking Hebrew. This is in comparison to native Hebrews who cannot speak Greek. In contrast, the KJV uses the less precise term "Grecians".

Acts 6:1 Now about this time, when the number of disciples was increasing, a complaint was made by the Hellenists (Greek-speaking Jews) against the [native] Hebrews because their widows were being overlooked in the daily serving of food. AMP

This verse discusses the new reality in the Judaism of biblical times. Many Jewish people found work in outposts of the Greek and Roman empires. Their ability to speak Greek, as well as the local language, made them invaluable intermediaries. The Romans relied on them to communicate with the local population. Some worked as traders for similar reasons. Alexandria was the largest of these Greek Speaking outposts.

Some dispute the contention of Droysen and others that Hellenism started with Alexander the Great. They argue that the cultural influence of Greece was visible in the East before Alexander's expeditions. This was especially true in Phoenicia and Egypt. According to Hengel, this latter view is becoming the more widely accepted consensus. (72) To provide a historical context, the return of the Jewish nation from their Babylonian exile began in 538 BC. Upon their return, the Jewish people sought to restore their national identity and follow their law more closely. At the death of Alexander the Great in 321BC, the combined forces of Macedonia and Greece were stretched virtually halfway around the known world. From Egypt in the West to Northwest India in the East. The territory Alexander conquered included Persia and Gaza. Once they were overcome militarily, the process of Hellenization was used to contain this great variety of cultures. By filling these cultures with Greek language and influence, these nations often lost much of their initial identity.

The nation of Israel was not immune to this process of being introduced to the Greek language and customs as a means of societal control. Young Hebrew men began to speak in Greek, a language that was supposed to provide culture and sophistication. They started to dress in togas and went to gymnasiums where the main attraction was naked wrestling matches. Distinctive aspects of Hebrew culture were gradually being abandoned. The Greek strategy was sophisticated and did not forbid the Jewish religion.

Yet, Hellenization saw the Jewish religion gradually lose favour, as some thought of it as old-fashioned and ineffective. (73)

One of the most important aspects of the Hellenization of Judaism was the Hebrew Scriptures being translated into Greek around 250 to 100 BC. The result was the Septuagint. According to the records of the time, there were seventy-two Jewish scholars commissioned by Ptolemy II Philadelphus, who was a Greek Pharaoh. Ptolemy II wanted the Hebrew Scriptures translated into Greek so they could be included in the Library of Alexandria. The translation of the Old Testament into Greek and the way the New Testament was recorded in Greek have effectively changed the way the Scriptures have been understood.

This book seeks to be an introduction to the potential of Hebrew thinking to change your view of Scripture. One aspect of the emergence of Hellenization was that it increased the separation between the Pharisees and the Sadducees. The Pharisees were mostly from the lower classes and saw Hellenization as something to be resisted. The Pharisees presented themselves as the protectors of true Judaism. Pharisees believe in the reality of the spiritual world as well as the need to keep Jewish traditions. The Pharisees were thought of as being closer to the people.

Alternatively, the Sadducees rejected notions of spirituality and miracles and felt more at home with the humanism inherent in Greek thought. The Sadducees found much in common with the Hellenizers and were promoted to positions of authority. The Sadducees were aristocrats and hereditary priests appointed to manage Jerusalem's temple. (74) Despite seeking to present themselves as being independent of Hellenization, it significantly influenced the Pharisees. They adopted a student-teacher relationship that was derived from the Hellenistic worldview and not found in Jewish thinking. The Pharisees also transformed the synagogue into a university for Jewish learning, a place to read from the Torah, study, sing and pray. While the Sadducees adopted an aristocratic demeanour, the Pharisees had discussions and scholarly debates about the true meaning of Judaic laws.

Antiochus IV (c215BC -164BC) was a ruler of The Greek Seleucid dynasty. He saw Judaism as a weak religion that was already largely assimilated into Greek thinking. To suppress and humiliate the Jewish people, Antiochus IV ordered the Jews to make unclean sacrifices in 167 BC. He banned all Mosaic ceremonial observances and demanded Jews eat the flesh of pigs. He is seen by many as the first type of antichrist and he demanded that all Jews worship him and the God Zeus in the Temple of Jerusalem. This is arguably the first example of the abomination of desolation, as referred to in the book of Daniel (75). You can read about this in the International Standard Bible Encyclopaedia online (76).

The actions of Antiochus IV started a revolt among the Jews in the town of Modiin, about 15 miles from Jerusalem. There the Government legate demanded that Mattathias, an ageing priest, perform the defiled sacrifice which he refused to do. As another Jew stepped forward to perform the demanded sacrifice, Mattathias killed him and the legate. He then smashed the altar and so began his life in hiding with his five sons. Mattathias and his followers were called Maccabees. They conducted a guerilla war for twenty years against the oppressive rule of Antiochus IV and his successors.

Mattathias died in 166 BC, and then his third son, Judas Maccabeus, took over as leader of the rebellion. Over the following six years, until his death, Judas led the vastly outnumbered forces of the Maccabees. After this, his brothers Jonathan and Simon took over. They not only won the return of Jewish religious freedom, they eventually gained total independence for Israel in 143 BC. The influence of this period on the Jewish psyche is difficult to overestimate. In 24 years the Jewish people rose from a seemingly insignificant vassal state controlled by the Greek empire to a nation with a vision for political independence. The leader that provided most of the inspiration for this transformation was Judas Maccabeus. Judas was cast as the great liberator of Israel and all the aspiring liberators of Israel who followed him were compared to him. The leadership of his brothers, Jonathan and Simon, kept Israel in political and religious freedom until 63 BC when they were invaded by the Roman Empire (77).

In Jesus' time, the memory of Judas Maccabeus was still an inspiration for many in the Jewish population. They still dreamed of another political liberator who could put an end to the oppression of Roman rule. Jesus had no interest in starting a rebellion against Rome. Those Jews, including the zealots, were seeking another political liberator. For them, Jesus was a disappointment (78).

In this Jewish outpost under the control of Rome walked a man called Jesus who transformed the lives of many and reframed the world's understanding of faith and life. God appointed a mouthpiece to introduce Jesus to the world and even he had his doubts about Jesus. In Matthew 11:3, John the Baptist asked the question, "Are you the One?"

"Are You the Expected One (the Messiah), or should we look for someone else [who will be the promised One]?" AMP in Matthew 11:3

If John the Baptist could not comprehend the message and mission of Jesus, who could? It seems most of Israel, including John the Baptist, had their expectations for a Messiah influenced by Judas Maccabeus. The expectation was that the Messiah would bring political liberation and freedom. In the following verses (Matthew 11:4-5) Jesus re-frames those expectations.

4 Jesus answered and said to them, "Go and tell John the things which you hear and see: 5 The blind see and the lame walk; the lepers are cleansed and the deaf hear; the dead are raised up and the poor have the gospel preached to them. NKJV

Jesus is not bringing a political kingdom, His kingdom is spiritual. Paul explains the spiritual nature of the kingdom of God in two separate verses. (1 Corinthians 4:20)

1 Corinthians 4:20: For the kingdom of God is not in word but in power. NKJV.

Then Romans 14:17: for the kingdom of God is not eating and drinking, but righteousness and peace and joy in the Holy Spirit NKJV

7.2 Hellenization and Christianity.

Greek thinking and Jewish thinking are entirely different ways of looking at the world. One important difference is that Greek thinking imposes its own assumptions. The Gospel was Jewish, not Greek, but the Greek thinkers began to interpret the Gospels in their own metaphysical way. Since the passing of St. John in 100 AD, few Christians understood the gospels from a Hebrew thinking perspective. The church of the second century was transitioning from the apostolic teaching of the first century to the seemingly inevitable rise of Greek thinking.

7.3 Philo and Neo-Platonism.

The city of Alexandria supported a large Jewish population. The most famous of them was Philo (20BC-50AD) who sought to merge the Hebrew Scriptures with Greek Culture. In his book *The Rise of Christianity* W.H.C. Frend writes of Philo: "He was Greek to the core in his language, education, and manners, and his Bible was the Septuagint. For him, there was no incompatibility between Hellenism and Judaism. While accepting the Law as the infallibly revealed will of God to both Jews and Gentiles, he attempted to interpret it exclusively through the mirror of Greek philosophy"(79).

The Bible says that the God of the Bible reveals many things to those who seek Him. This first of many contrasts between Greek and biblical thinking. Philo was the first to integrate Greek ideas into Christianity. He lived in Alexandria and was the originator of Neo-Platonism. The first idea he added was the incomprehensibility of The Christian God which is a Greek concept used to interpret the God of the Hebrews (80).

Until the second century, the Church was almost exclusively made up of Jewish believers. Few of these early leaders had a Greek-style education or the ability to think in a Greek way. Unfortunately, by the time the Gentile world needed teaching to learn the Christian faith, there was a lack of men with the capacity to teach it. Paul and John were able to present the gospel to the Greeks on their own terms. Unfortunately, because of the persecution from Roman, Jewish and pagan sources, the influence of the apostles was as good as gone. Few understood the Gospel and biblical truths, which meant the influence of the disciples had virtually disappeared by the end of the second century.

Through its pervasive education system, Greek thinking invaded Christianity and brought with it the Greek love of metaphysics and argument. Ideas were analysed and dissected in a way that was completely alien to the perspective of Jewish thinking. Greek thinking seeks a reason for everything and a definition or label for every idea. Greek thinking wants every idea to be supported by the proofs of rhetoric as taught in Greek schools.

In Greek philosophy, there is a love of complexity and metaphysical theorising. This approach is entirely at odds with the writings of Moses and the prophets. These Hebrew writings focus on absolutes. The Gospels and the Scriptures all come with a setting, form, style and context that are distinctly Jewish and are firmly rooted in Hebrew thinking. It is only logical, therefore, that it takes a Hebrew perspective to understand the Bible. In other words, one must think like an ancient Hebrew to understand Scripture however, the dominance of Greek thinking in heathen cultures around the time of Jesus meant that most people interpreted the scriptures according to metaphysical theorising. This is the way of the Greek philosophers. (81)

7.4 Greek Thinking: Denying that God can be Known.

John 14:6 Jesus said to him, "I am the [only] Way [to God] and the [real] Truth and the [real] Life; no one comes to the Father but through Me. 7 If you had [really] known Me, you would also have known My Father. From now on you know Him, and have seen Him." AMP

John 16:2 They will put you out of the synagogues and make you outcasts. And a time is coming when whoever kills you will think that he is offering service to God. 3. And they will do these things because they have not known the Father or Me. AMP.

The initial challenge of Greek thinking is to challenge the idea that humanity can know God. The concept that God is essentially unknowable is very common in today's church. Yet this concept is in direct contradiction to the words of Jesus in John 14. It is not difficult to find this example of Biblical understanding being compromised by Greek thought. It is the first of many.

Chapter Eight

The Early Church

Polycarp (69-155) was the bishop of Smyrna from around 107 AD. He served until a pagan mob murdered him in 155 AD. Polycarp saw the transition between the Apostolic Age and the arrival of the age of the Apologists. Polycarp is known to have been deeply saddened by what he saw as the progress of apostasy. Later in his life, Polycarp reportedly said repeatedly "Oh good God, to what times hast thou spared me, that I must suffer such things!" (82) These are the words of a frustrated leader. Another significant church leader of the time was Papias the Bishop of Hierapolis. Many believe the same uprising that caused the death of Polycarp also killed Papias. Papias was like Polycarp in that he wanted the early Church to follow the Apostles and their adherence to Hebrew thinking. Justin Martyr (100-165 AD) lived in a time when Gnosticism was threatening to become the dominant form of Christianity. Justin fought against the Gnostics yet they shared some common values. These were a deep-seated anti-Jewish sentiment and a Greek philosophical approach to biblical interpretation. Gnostics like Marcion, or popular writings like the Epistle of Barnabas, sprang from these same Greek influences (83). Clement

of Alexandria (150-215AD) believed the reason Plato discovered
so much of the truth about God was due to his familiarity with the
writings of Moses. Greek philosophy may be theologically flawed,
but in Clement's view, its concepts were imbued with divine inspiration and insight linked directly to the Law.

Irenaeus (130-202AD) was the Most Renowned of the Greek
Apologists and although he received training from Polycarp as a
young boy, his knowledge of the gospels was lacking. This was
not because Irenaeus lacked intelligence, this was just a natural
consequence of the persecutions that the Church had to endure.
Polycarp was one of the few who had known the Apostles, but
he was not thought of as a great theologian. He was a bishop,
but not a philosopher. Polycarp did his best in a time of difficult
circumstances. When Irenaeus wrote to Florinus, he was thank-
ful for his study under Polycarp, but complained about his poor
recollection of Gospel principles and that he failed to write more
down. Indeed, in the second century written knowledge of Jesus
was almost entirely limited to the four Gospels. As a result, one
major difficulty the Apologists faced was limited knowledge of the
Christian message (84). Tertullian of Carthage (c 150-212) was the
church father most opposed to the influence of Greek philosophy
on the church. From this perspective, Tertullian asked his famous
question, " What does Athens have to do with Jerusalem?" (85)
Around 100 AD Clement, who was the overseer bishop of Rome,
sent a critical letter to the Corinthian church because they had
divisive factions. Clement encouraged the Corinthians to restore
their pure faith and restore leaders of the church who the con-
gregation had previously removed. Clement described the Old
Testament as "sacred Scriptures". At this time the authority of

the Hebrew writings was still accepted. In the following decades, there would be heated disputes about the relevance of the Hebrew Scriptures for Christians (86). At the time the fourth century arrived, Greek culture began to dominate. At this time Christian converts began to read the bible less and Christian writers referred to Scripture less frequently. There is an example of Father Basil, who wrote to his old teacher Libanius in the fourth century, saying, "I must apologise for the style of this letter. The truth is, I have been in the company of Moses and Elias, and men of that kind, who tell us no doubt what is true, but in a barbarous dialect so that your instructions have quite gone out of my head." (101) Many Protestants believe their adherence to the principle of Sola Scriptura has allowed them to escape dogma in the form of false traditions. The traditional belief is that dogma has been left behind at the door of the Roman Church. This belief is very common in many protestant denominations.

8.1 The Apologists: Polycarp.

With the passing of both Polycarp and Papias, the influence of Greek philosophy began to dominate the church. The church had lost its original strong leadership and Greek thinking became more influential. By the time of the passing of Polycarp, Greek thinking dominated the church. As a consequence, an entirely new theology was created. Greek thinking meant that the church's understanding of God became radically different to the biblical revelation and the Hebrew thinking of the apostles. The estimated date that 1

Corinthians was written c. 55AD (87). In chapter 13 of this book, Paul's argument that Greek philosophy is incompatible with spirituality is outlined. It was only a little more than 100 years on that these instructions were largely forgotten and the church continued on its path towards being dominated by Greek thinking.

8.2 The Apologists: Justin Martyr.

Justin Martyr was called the first apologist by numerous historians. Justin came to Christianity after having made a thorough study of Greek philosophy. This study included the philosophies of the Peripatetics or the school of Aristotle, the Pythagoreans, the Stoics, and Plato. Despite Justin's study of Greek scholars and his role as an apologist for Greek thinking, he was not especially single-minded in his promotion of Greek thinking. Justin was convinced in his own way that aspects of Greek philosophy were incorrect. He was deeply impressed with the Old Testament prophets and the life and death of Jesus Christ.

Justin Martyr was raised as a pagan in a Jewish environment in Palestine with Philosophy being a major part of his education. At the age of 32, he converted to Christianity, possibly in Ephesus. Around the age of 35, became an itinerant preacher. Moving between cities in the Roman Empire, Justin attempted to bring educated pagans to Christ by continuing to teach philosophy and discuss Christianity. As discussed before, Justin Martyr did not take a simplistic approach, however, he did believe that a synthesis between philosophy and Christianity would benefit Christianity. Justin hoped that his reasoning and analysis of the Greek philosophers would help his apologetics. He hoped that by learning the Greek language and their philosophy, he could help Greeks understand the Bible (88).

8.3 The Apologists: Clement.

Clement was strongly influenced by his teacher Justin Martyr. He believed Christianity was the true philosophy and was not opposed to Greek philosophy but was in fact the fulfilment of it. For Clement the best of Greek thought such as Socrates and Plato was helpful for Christian thinkers. Clement saw Greek philosophy as the way to bring the "Hellenic mind" to Christ much the same way Paul said the Law was given to bring Jews to Christ. "Accordingly, before the advent of the Lord, philosophy was necessary to the Greeks for righteousness.

For Hans van Campenhausen, a German professor of church history, Clement was" almost the prototype of a liberal theologian" Clement of Alexandria sought to integrate the Christian faith with the learning of the day (89). Clement did not accept every Greek idea and he certainly rejected the notion that the universe is eternal despite it being the view of every major Greek philosopher. Olson describes Clement as an early version of Paul Tillich (1886-1965) who was a German philosophical theologian who sought to create harmony among diverse views (90).

Ultimately, a number of the leading Apologists left the church. For example, after Justin Martyr died, his student Tatian became a radical Gnostic. Tertullian left the Church around 200AD with what he believed were strong doctrinal objections. Yet, both these writers are still considered eminent Christian teachers of the time. It was inevitable that eventually the Apologists would be influenced by their opposition to anti-Christian writers and heretics. Irenaeus, Tertullian and Origen were all prodigious writers. These writers all wrote largely against heresy, but this heresy was coming as a tidal wave. It was inevitable that some error would creep into their thinking specifically and the church in general. (91).

During this period, and continuing into the next century, official Roman persecution of Christians flared and ebbed, but never completely died out. There were severe persecutions during the reigns of Marcus Aurelius (161-180), Decius (249-238), Valerian (253-260) and Diocletian (284-305) all attempted to eradicate any groups that declared themselves to be Christian. Throughout the third century there was an environment of competition with other Christian sects, and battles with Gnosticism. Ultimately, it was Hellenised Christianity that came to dominate and eventually they defined what is orthodox (92).

8.4 Apologists: Irenaeus.

When Irenaeus (130-202) first encountered Gnosticism, his response was anything but detached and rational. Irenaeus sought to expose Gnosticism both for its fundamental incoherence and its negative attitude towards the material world. Irenaeus argued that this teaching was heretical. Irenaeus' critique was largely responsible for Gnosticism becoming a belief system that was understood to be heretical by both biblical and apostolic standards. For Irenaeus, Gnosticism was a complete corruption of the gospel, yet it came in the disguise of superior wisdom for spiritual people.

8.5 Tertullian.

Tertullian has been described as similar to an early Karl Barth (1886-1968) who sought to produce a mode of Christian thinking untainted by paganism. Tertullian was pessimistic about the human capacity to avoid syncretism and idolatry. He warned believers to stay away from the study of too much philosophy lest they be seduced by heresy. One of the targets of Tertullian's most critical writing was Marcion the Gnostic. Tertullian explained many Christian beliefs in ways that were new. Tertullian desired to explain the true meaning and implications of orthodox faith (93). The role of philosophy in Christian thought is accepted by most today, yet as per Tertullian's famous question, he saw philosophy as the cause of heresy among Christians.

For many of today's students of theology, the statements of Tertullian may seem unreasonable as he speaks out against philosophy and philosophers. It should be remembered that Tertullian was speaking out against syncretism which was fast becoming the standard of the apologists amongst others (94). In his arguments against this syncretism, Tertullian was known to quote Colossians 2:8.

Colossians 2:8 See to it that no one takes you captive through philosophy and empty deception [pseudo-intellectual babble], according to the tradition [and musings] of mere men, following the elementary principles of this world, rather than following [the truth-the teachings of] Christ. AMP

Tertullian wrote his paraphrased version: "See that no one beguile you through philosophy and vain deceit, after the tradition of men, and contrary to the wisdom of the Holy Spirit." (95) This statement of Tertullian can be described as very reasonable and Biblical, yet, Tertullian has been considered by opponents to be a promoter of irrationality. As Arthur Klem has written, " Tertullian is customarily pictured as teaching that faith, in order to be genuinely Christian, must contradict human reason." (96) There is nothing irrational in his paraphrasing of Colossians 2:8.

Tertullian developed his well-known opposition to philosophers because they had widespread differences of opinion and their scepticism was unwarranted. Arthur Klem, an Evangelical theologian, describes Tertullian's objections to philosophy as having "a perspective of objectivity for which he is not ordinarily credited", further that "Most of what he (Tertullian) says about philosophy and philosophers is negative, but it does not follow that this opposition is blind, unreasoned or merely subjective." (97)

There is much that Tertullian wrote about that is outside the scope of this book. Arthur Klem concludes after an academic study of all of his writings by saying, "that Tertullian cannot rightly be called anti-rational. It is true that he seems to be guilty of various kinds of extremism, violent expression, inconsistencies, etc., but there is nothing remarkable in that. Tertullian's outlook and emphases are clearly rational." (98)

Is it possible that Tertullian's main offence is that he highlighted Paul's Scriptural warning that the Christian faith, and Greek philosophy, were incompatible? Not only does this fit the facts but it also seems to fit the general tenor of academic criticism regarding Hebrew thought (as seen in chapter 10), as well as academic criticism of Paul himself (as seen in sections 13.5 & 13.6).

Eventually, Tertullian was overwhelmed by apostate views and he left the church for Montanism (99).

8.6 The church 100 to 300.

As the second century arrived, Christianity was going through profound changes. The influence of the original apostles was waning and individual local groups began to develop their own teachings and practices. Non-Jewish converts brought new influences that were sometimes pagan into the churches. There were debates about what was correct doctrine and required for religious observance as well as the debate about choosing the books for the canon of Scripture. There were also additional issues like how should people understand who Jesus was and his significance.

As the church approached 200AD, Christianity was in transition. The first century saw controversy focused on issues like Jewish sectarianism and circumcision. The conflicts of the second century moved to disputes about Gnosticism, Hellenism and paganism. Jesus' apostles and earliest disciples understood that the Hebrew Scriptures were literal instructions from God. The second century saw Christians starting to interpret the Scriptures allegorically. W.H.C. Frend in *The Rise of Christianity* describes the period between 135, the year of the second fall of Jerusalem up until this year of 200 AD as a time of "...great changes in the organization of the church and the outlook of its members." (100) This scenario of uncertainty became the breeding ground for this new Hellenistic orthodoxy.

The dominant culture of the world at this time was Hellenism. Greek philosophy and education had become the basis of the education systems. The Apologists and many Christians of the time had Greek thinking as the foundation of their theological learning. This was true for the apologists and the heretics. This all was in contrast with the Scriptures which were written on the assumptions of the Hebrew prophets. At this time the possibility that interpreting Scriptures through the lens of Greek philosophy would lead to inaccuracy was a concept largely limited to Tertullian. For the great majority, it was not an issue worthy of consideration.

The impact of this transition between Hebrew thinking and Greek thinking had its beginnings in the early church and has continued largely unabated until today. As time passed from the time of the apostles and their memory faded, the literal understanding that the Old Testament brings also started to fade. A new orthodoxy began to emerge. Pagans were being converted to Hellenised Christianity. This syncretic mix of the Bible with Greek philosophy became the preferable expression of Christianity in a world which was dominated by Greek thought. As W.H.C. Frend points out, "For two centuries the relationship between Platonism and Christianity oscillated between attraction and repulsion. Basically, nothing could be more opposed than the Jewish and Greek view of God, of creation, of time and history, and of the role of humanity in the universe." (101)

What changed this view was that the views of Philo, The Alexandrian Gnostics and Clement were all beginning to combine and produce a faith that was pagan-friendly. The new version of biblical understanding came through the lens of Platonic thinking (102).

8.7 The church 300 to 400 on.

The Greeks also loved Sophistry. Sophistry is the philosophy behind advanced speech and rhetoric. It is where the word sophisticated comes from. Greek thinkers have a preference for professional teachers and preachers. This preference was adopted by the church and preaching replaced teaching. Christian church leaders were expected to communicate with sophistication to their church. Through the dominance of Greek education, Greek thought invaded Christianity. Greek education in the church helped to develop a mix of the Christian faith with Greek-style arguments and metaphysics. Church leaders began to analyse ideas in ways that were absolutely foreign to Jewish thinking. (103) Greek thinking seeks a reason for everything and seeks to label and define each and every idea. Greek thinking seeks evidence and proof to support its ideas.

8.8 The Status of Sola Scriptura.

The Catholic church openly admits that God has instituted what they describe as sacred traditions which may vary from the Bible. The Protestant churches claim to be different in that they strictly adhere to Scripture. The problem is that the theology of the Protestant church is so deeply grounded and interpreted through philosophical thought, that its connection with biblical truth is much weaker than is generally understood. (104) Greek-style interpretation strongly influenced the church from the second century on. Many of the conflicts that are debated in contemporary theology had their beginnings at this time. These false doctrines became embedded in the thinking of the church. Since then crucial errors have come to define protestant theology in virtually every denomination. (105)

Chapter Nine

The Influence of Augustine

A t the end of the fourth-century theological apostasy in the church was deep-seated. Enter Augustine, who, with others, organised opinions about God so they were easily understood. Augustine (354-430 AD), was the most prominent theologian in the 4th Century Church, but he was far more than that. After a time of persecution and uncertainty in the world, Augustine began to be prominent in the church. He was known as a great orator and taught at a range of universities. His place in history is incredibly important. He is one of the last really influential theologians prior to the middle ages. He is known as the last of the ancient Christian writers and the forerunner of mediaeval theology. Augustine influenced John Calvin and most of 16th-century Protestant theology. In the 1200s Thomas Aquinas sought to accommodate the work of Aristotle within the church. This Thomistic Scholasticism brought together reason-based and revelation-based thinking into a new acceptable whole. He did this by dividing the world into two distinct realms: the realm of nature and the realm of grace. Grace includes anything to do with the supernatural including God, angels, prayer and worship. Alternatively, there is the natural realm which includes science, logic and economics. These are matters to do with the natural and material realms. This meant that Aquinas defined a world that was separated between the secular realm and the natural realm. In the mind of Aquinas, these two realms were never in opposition to each other. However, by the 1700s the Enlightenment began to dominate academic life in Europe. The Enlightenment focused on anything material and scientific while disregarding the spiritual. These ideas are still influential today and Aquinas opened up the doorway for western science. (106) John Calvin (1509 - 1564) was a pastor, theologian and reformer. Calvin established his academy in Geneva, Switzerland, and protestants from all over Europe flocked there. Reformers like John Knox (1514-1572) made Calvinism synonymous with Reformed theology in the English-speaking world. The Puritans of England considered themselves Calvinists, and so did the Puritans of New England. Calvinism came to be known to be the label of choice for most of Europe's Reformed churches even though there were differences between them. The terms Reformed and Calvinist are similar but not exactly identical, yet Calvin's great work *Institutes of Christian Religion* became the textbook for reformed theology for hundreds of years to come. (107)

9.1 Augustine.

Augustine was well known for the way he promoted Platonic philosophy (108). After Augustine converted to Christianity, his writings sought to show that Platonic philosophy was essentially correct and that Platonic thinking helped the church understand biblical truth. Bishop Ambrose was one of the most influential figures of the church in the early 4th century. Ambrose was intellectual and articulate, which helped convince Augustine to be a Christian. Shortly after Augustine's conversion, Ambrose baptised him. Augustine wrote of Ambrose's father, saying ..."he congratulated me because I had not fallen in with the writings of other philosophers, full of fallacies and deceits according to the elements of this world, whereas in the works of the Platonists, God and His word are introduced in all manners. " (109)

Augustine wrote influential books such as *The City of God, On Christian Doctrine and Confessions*. Augustine interpreted St Paul from the perspective of Platonic philosophy in a way that is still influencing Christianity today. That is because the academic world has always been dominated by Greek philosophy and, as has been outlined the capacity of the apostles to define our understanding of the Scriptures was relatively short-lived. (110) The Platonist understanding of Scripture that started with Philo was later refined by the Apologists. This understanding became the orthodox understanding of the Scriptures under the church leadership of Augustine. The Biblical revelation was interpreted by the main doctrines of Plato. Many doctrines from Greek philosophy were absorbed into orthodox Christian thinking. There was a time when it was quite common for people to refer to Socrates and Plato as "Christians before Christ." Many Christians seriously believed that the historic mission of those Greek thinkers had been to prepare the theoretical foundations for some important aspects of Christianity. The detailed working out of these connections was something that preoccupied many scholars during the Middle Ages. Plato, to state the obvious, was neither Christian nor Jew and arrived at his conclusions in complete independence of the Judeo-Christian tradition. In fact, he arrived at them by philosophical argument. (111)

The church fathers before him believed in and taught God's supremacy and the human soul's dependency on grace, but Augustine contributed a new spin to those ideas: a concept called monergism. This is the idea that human agency is passive and it is only the agency of God that determines history and whether individuals are saved or not. These ideas, especially concepts like the depravity of man and predestination have been linked to the 16th-century protestant John Calvin. The broader perspective of Augustine's monergistic idea is that history and salvation are determined solely by God. (112)

Prior to Augustine, Christian theology was dominated by a view called synergism which believes that human agency and God's agency cooperate in some way so they can produce both history and salvation. While Augustine stated he believed in the concept of human freedom, all of his thinking argues against any genuine freedom for humanity. For Augustine God always gets his way, even when humans act sinfully. (113)

In Carthage, prior to him becoming a Christian, Augustine came under the influence of a new cult known as Manichaeism.

The Manichaeans followed a Persian prophet named Manes who was martyred by the Romans. Augustine was attracted to the Manichaeans because they seemed intellectual and offered what he thought were superior answers to those offered either by Christianity or traditional paganism. The Manichaeans believed that there were two eternal and equally powerful forces the sources of good and evil that engaged in endless combat. Similar to the Gnostics they believed there was an evil force controlling matter and creation whereas the good God of heaven created what was spiritual and good. Initially, Augustine believed they solved the mystery of evil, but eventually, he became disillusioned with Manichaeism and he moved to Rome and Milan (114).

Augustine began teaching rhetoric at the Academy in Milan where he lived as a pagan. Augustine came under two significant influences, the first was Neo-Platonism, which helped him develop his arguments against the Manichaeans. Eventually, Augustine came to believe that Christianity could not answer the problem of evil which asks how can you explain the existence of evil if God is all-powerful as well as perfectly good. Why is there so much evil in the world that God created out of nothing? Did not God have to create evil then? Does this not make God the author of evil? Augustine's solution to the problem of evil was that it was not the creation of God but was the corruption of that nature. Neo-Platonism is a pagan philosophy yet it gave Augustine a key that helped him unlock the door enabling him to enter his mother's Christian faith (115). Despite the fact, there is no Neo-Platonic conception of a personal God Augustine believed it was less dangerous and more useful for the gospel than Manichaeism.

A second influence on Augustine was his debate with Pelagius (c.350 - c. 423) which helped Augustine develop his concept of salvation. Pelagius arrived in Rome around 405 where he was disturbed by the level of immorality amongst professing Christians living there. For Pelagius, the grace of God's Word and a Christian's conscience is enough to allow them to live a sinless life. Augustine believed in the absolute depravity of mankind after the fall as well as the total sovereignty of God. He wrote six or more books responding to the broader issues of salvation (116). Augustine believed that humans are so depraved that they need the gift of faith by grace, or else they would never be able to even think of something good.

Augustine's views extended to a refutation of Pelagius' as well as all forms of synergism, which is the belief that humanity and God are mutually responsible for salvation. Pelagius was eventually condemned as a heretic. As Olson says "Augustine's view of original sin and human depravity is as strong as any can possibly be. According to Him, all humans alive at any given time (with the sole exception of the God-man Jesus Christ) are included in a 'mass of perdition' and are altogether guilty and damned by God on account of Adam's primal sin" (117)

These are ideas without compromise. To underline the significance of this view, Roger Olson summarises the view of Augustine scholar T. Kermitt Scott as " The key to understanding Augustine is his obsession with the absolute and unconditional power of God." (118) In Scott's own words, "The omnipotence doctrine is the heart of Augustine's imperial myth, and when "push comes to shove" it is the doctrine that cannot be compromised. God is the absolute ruler of the universe whose will directs every event in creation. That fundamental certainty cannot be qualified in any way regardless of the consequences it may have." (119)

The logical ramifications of the extreme nature of this view are breathtaking. Despite the fact Augustine refused to acknowledge it, the logical corollary to his view has to be that God created evil. To consistently apply these ideas of Augustine means that of necessity God must be behind the holocaust, the death of every innocent child and every cruel and unjust event in human history. Think about that. To believe Augustine is to believe that every cancer and every act of war that has killed and injured children have all been caused directly at the instigation of God. (120)

Such an extreme view could, in other circumstances, be considered delusional but it is the core belief of Augustine who is an extremely intelligent man. A man who " was hailed by virtually all the popes and the major Protestant reformers as the greatest of the church fathers." (121)

So let us try and get some perspective on this situation. After the decline of the apostolic influence came a time of church persecution and instability. After 312 when Emperor Constantine had an experience he believed came from God, the Empire became more tolerable for Christians. Into this era of relative stability came Augustine and his influential views. Being modelled on Neo-Platonism and Greek philosophy meant they automatically had a level of acceptance. While the worldwide church claims to base all its beliefs on Scripture, they have been interpreted through the lens of Greek philosophy. As a consequence faith has been taken in a direction that was opposite to the original Hebrew beliefs of the apostolic fathers.

When we summarise the influence of Augustine we can point to three key ideas. These ideas are all ultimately derived from Greek thinking and each of them varies from Scripture in profound ways.

Throughout Augustine's life, he constantly insisted that only God was the ultimate cause of all things. In his book "*The Story of Christian Theology*", Roger Olson, quoted the Augustine scholar T.Kermit Scott who confirms the truth of this statement. At the risk of repetition, Olson writes "Scott is quite correct that in the final analysis the key to understanding Augustine is his obsession with the absolute and unconditional power of God." (122) As a historical principle, Augustine's concept of a controlling God became inserted into the foundations of Western Christianity. Most theologians and historians are in agreement that the dominant force of Christian thought has been Augustine. (123)

Harold Eberle, and his book (2009) *Christianity Unshackled*, identifies these 3 key ideas that define Augustine's thought. These ideas have influenced Christian thinking over the centuries.

1. "God is in control

2. Humanity is inherently evil

3. This world is inherently corrupt." (124)

In addition to these three statements from Eberle, this book argues that Augustine promoted a fourth defining belief. The main influences on Augustine were the writings of Plotinus, (204-270 AD) and Porphyry (c.234 -305 AD) from which he learned about Neo-Platonism. Plotinus, Porphyry and the Greek philosophers taught that the spiritual realm was the real world and the natural realm was much less important and considered evil. Western Christianity has come to largely believe in this separation between the natural and spiritual worlds, a view that has been derived from Platonic dualism and was emphasised by Thomas Aquinas. (125)

9.2 The Dualism of Thomas Aquinas.

In the 1200s Thomas Aquinas sought to accommodate the work of Aristotle within the church. This Thomistic Scholasticism brought together reason-based and revelation-based thinking into a new acceptable whole. He did this by dividing the world into two distinct realms: the realm of nature and the realm of grace. Grace includes anything to do with the supernatural including God, angels, prayer and worship. Alternatively, there is the natural realm which includes science, logic and economics. These are matters to do with the natural and material realms. This meant that Aquinas defined a world that was separated between the secular realm and the natural realm. In the mind of Aquinas, these two realms were never in opposition to each other. However, by the 1700s the Enlightenment began to dominate academic life in Europe. The Enlightenment focused on anything material and scientific while disregarding the spiritual. These ideas are still influential today and Aquinas opened up the doorway for western science. (126)

9.3 Calvinism.

Calvin's doctrine of God followed the teachings of Augustine, as Calvin taught that God was the ultimate cause of everything. Calvin also taught that nothing can happen unless God determines it. He wrote in his Institutes "The first man fell because the lord had judged it to be expedient; why is so judged is hidden from us. Yet it is certain that he has so judged because he saw that there by the glory of his name is duly revealed" (127).

Calvin also said, "For as Augustine truly contends, they also measure divine justice by the standard of human justice are acting perversely"(128). John Calvin built his theology on the ideas of Augustine who taught that all events are covered by God's secret plan. Augustine and Calvin have depicted our loving Heavenly Father as in control of everything. There is no mention or acknowledgement of the reality of evil. Nor, is there the biblical understanding that Jesus healed all who were oppressed by the devil as in Acts 10:38.

Acts 10:38 how God anointed Jesus of Nazareth with the Holy Spirit and with power, who went about doing good and healing all who were oppressed by the devil, for God was with Him. NKJV.

The biblical account is unambiguous, Jesus and the Holy Spirit consistently free people from oppression and bring healing whenever the devil is found to be oppressing people with sickness or mental illness. Calvinism says little about evil. This theology believes that God executes everything whether it is good or evil. (129)

Chapter Ten

Academic Thinking.

A significant and influential group of modern thinkers argue that the Greek language and thinking have not affected the modern church. Some scholars also argue that Greek thinking has helped Christianity and not led it away from biblical values. In the early 20th century the linguist Benjamin Whorf wrote theories that James Barr opposed vigorously. Benjamin Lee Whorf (1897-1941) was an American and one of the most influential thinkers in linguistics. He wrote that there is a relationship between the structure of a language and the thinking of those who speak it. Whorf is often linked with Edward Sapir (1884-1939) and the theory that language influences thought is called the Sapir-Whorf hypothesis. (130) In his book, *The Semantics of Biblical Language* (1961) James Barr made his critical statement opposing the tendency of theologians of the time to argue that language reveals the underlying worldview of a culture. Barr objects to any theological perspective that seeks to find a worldview in the vocabulary of a language. Barr is also critical of those who seek to come to a deeper understanding of Scripture by analysing the Hebrew language. Barr is aggressive in placing his knowledge and experience in support of the idea that Greek thinking is the natural environment of the New Testament. As a consequence, many have believed that the exploration of Hebraic thinking has little to offer Biblical scholarship. Dr Dru Johnson is an associate professor of biblical and Theological studies at Kings College in New York City. Johnson wrote in 2019 that "Last century, a robust debate about the nature of Hebrew mentality (i.e., how they actually thought) eventually became known as the Hebrew-Greek mind problem .... that debate ended in academia with a fairly definitive loss for those who maintained the Hebrew-Greek dichotomy." (131) For academics like Johnson, the winner of this debate was Barr. The key issue that this book seeks to explore is the dominance of Greek thinking in Bible translations and church practice and the influence this has had. The first effect is that key Hebrew understandings have been suppressed or distorted.

10.1 The Influence of Greek Thought.

Dr Dru Johnson an associate professor of biblical and Theological studies at Kings College in New York City, wrote an article, (2019) *Did Ancient Hebrews have different minds from the Greeks?* (132) which is about what he describes as the previous century's debate regarding the Hebrew mind. This debate was eventually called the Hebrew-Greek mind problem. According to Dr Johnson, that debate ended in the academic world with "a fairly definitive loss for those who maintained the Hebrew-Greek dichotomy". (133) This meant that Dru Johnson and academics who share his opinion consider that the differences between the Hebrew mind and the Greek mind are inconsequential. (134)

James Barr's unfavourable appraisal of these two-mind constructs has been adopted by many academics, including Dru Johnson. Barr grouped the two-mind proposals by the following properties: 1) the contrast of Greek thinking as stative and Hebrew as dynamic, 2) the contrast of Greek thinking as abstract and Hebrew as concrete, and 3) the contrast of the Greek conception of man as a duality and the Hebrew conception of a unitary being.

Barr's basic rejoinder aims to disprove the claim that two distinct mentalities can be derived from the languages of the people represented. While Hebrew represents the "verb" mentality and Greek the "noun," Barr asks if this dichotomy is a reflection of the mentality of the people, or is it simply the nature of the texts. Barr argues for the latter, pointing out the phenomenological aspect of the extant texts: "The typical vehicle of Hebrew thinking is the historical narrative or the future prediction, both forms of literature in which the verb is likely to be of great significance." (135) His second major critique points to the vague nature of the comparison itself.

Academics like Johannes Pedersen argue that the difference is a function of the Israelite people and the texts were reflecting these human differences. He argued that the Israelites only spoke and thought about the things that they saw or perceived directly. The Israelites did not think about things abstractly therefore they did not have the language to discuss beliefs that are entirely alien to their mindset. According to Pedersen, the Israelites do not occupy themselves with empty nor with sharply defined concepts. Their logic is not the logic of abstraction, but of immediate perception.

It is characteristic that the problems treated in the Old Testament are problems pertaining not to thought, but to life, and that what they seek are not logical results. (136)

For Pedersen, the Hebrew mind unites concepts so that a man can only conceive of action and outcome as a unity, not a cause and effect which demands further investigation. For the Israelites, "there is no such thing as 'good intentions'" because "the intention or will is identical with the totality of the soul which creates action" (137). Pedersen argues that this inability to abstract means that ancient Hebrews could not think as we do. Their thoughts focused on what is tangible and active, whereas ours can freely range in the abstract world of ideas.

In a comparative study, Thorlief Boman explains the contrast between Israelite and Greek thinking by arguing for a dynamic/stative dichotomy. While the Israelites only think in terms of dynamic action, Greeks developed the ability to think of bodies and properties as stative concepts now domesticated by their minds. (138)

In making the case, Boman argues that Hebrew thought was fundamentally psychological while Greek thought was logical. Logical, in this sense, means the ability to place "ourselves objectively and impersonally outside the matter and ask what is the strict truth about it."(139) As for the psychological Hebrew mind, "psychic life, thinking and understanding are inseparable." And, "when we would understand a matter psychologically, we familiarise ourselves with it and through the sympathetic pursuit of its development we try to grasp it as a necessity."(140) Hebrew thought in some ways is not really thinking at all, but reacting to an environment.

10.2 The No Problem example

To illustrate this from a personal viewpoint, I lived in China from 2002 to 2008 and immediately after that, I lived in Hong Kong until 2013. While I am far from a fluent speaker of Chinese and my experience of the Chinese language is very limited, I have seen significant ways in which the vocabulary and structure of the Chinese language reflect Chinese culture. For example, one of the most important principles of Chinese culture is that people need to avoid what is called loss of face. This means doing something that brings the negative opinion of others. Traditional Chinese culture emphasises unity and harmony, and loss of face is something to be avoided at all costs.

One common expression in English, especially in Australia, is "no problem". This is where there is a potentially problematic interaction between people. Instead of being upset, one party declares "no problem". The focus is on the potential issue and it is declared to be insignificant. Within this statement, the priority of Western culture can be observed. That priority is the focus on the idea or the potential problem, rather than making a statement about the people concerned. This approach adopts the emphasis of Greek thought where the focus is on thinking and ideas.

Alternatively, in the Chinese language, the expression that is normally used in this situation is "mei guanxi" which in simplest English means "No Problem". Guanxi means relationship and is typically used to describe the positive relationship that is needed for business deals. Mei guanxi means no relationship or this issue will not be a negative influence on our relationship. There is a clear contrast. In English, the focus is the idea or the problem whereas, in Chinese, the focus is the relationship. This is a clear example of cultural priorities and worldviews that can be seen in language and in a similar way this is an example of language providing insights into differing worldviews.

If I can find examples in the Chinese language from my limited knowledge, then it seems surprising to me that this idea is not better supported in the academic world. My experience in China, and the study I have made of the language and thinking of the Hebrew Scriptures (discussed further in chapter 11), all point to a significance of language beyond anything that seems to be recognised by those who adopt the views of James Barr. The late James Barr (1924-2006) has been the main challenger to the arguments of the Sapir-Whorf hypothesis. Barr wrote an extremely influential book in 1961 called *The Semantics of Biblical Language*. (141) In this book, he outlined his argument that the Hebrew language was not significant in helping people understand Hebrew biblical texts. Barr was an influential academic and he held the position of Regus professor of Hebrew at Oxford University from 1978 to 1989. (142)

Barr explains his objections in his book *From Biblical Faith and Natural Theology* (1993) where he wrote about the nature of Paul's thinking. Barr starts with a scriptural reading of Acts 17:16-34 which recounts an evangelistic speech Paul made to the men of Athens at Areopagus. Barr argues Paul is developing a version of natural theology which he describes as argumentative thinking designed to prove the existence of God from the nature of the world around us. Natural theology follows the model of Greek thinking and logic. As Barr states, "Paul's speech is distinctly friendly to Greek thought and displays no polemic in principle against it. He moves unembarrassedly within its language, terms, and categories—just as other Jewish thinkers of Greek speech did." (143)

Barr argues that this is an example of Greek thinking embedded in Scripture so he comes to the conclusion that Greek thinking and Scripture cannot be mutually exclusive. This is the only reference Barr provides in the chapter before making this statement, "I also think, though I shall not attempt to prove it in detail, that much of the New Testament, and especially of the letters, and most of all of the Pauline letters, is much more Greek in its terms, its conceptuality, and its thinking than main trends of modern biblical theology have tended to allow. My own experience makes this to me undeniable. If one has spent most of one's life, as I have, working on Hebrew and other Semitic-language texts, and then returns after some absence to a closer study of the New Testament, the impression of the essentially Greek character of the latter is overwhelming, and especially so in St Paul, much less so in some other areas like the teaching of Jesus as seen in the Synoptic Gospels. The attempt, at one time popular and influential, to argue that, though the words might be Greek, the thought processes were fundamentally Hebraic, was a conspicuous failure." (144)

Here Barr is being heavy-handed and using his personal academic status to justify that opinion. It is one thing to say that Paul's speech to the Greeks is full of Greek thinking, but Barr extrapolates that specific reference to argue that much of the New Testament is "overwhelming" in its Greek character. While the initial reference may well be valid, the breadth of his extrapolation is without evidence or, in my estimation, substance. This speech is the only evidence Barr provides in this book. This speech was specifically made for the very defined purpose of communicating the gospel to the Greeks and it was designed to communicate within a Greek thinking frame of reference. That Paul would seek to make his speech understandable to his audience is a measure of his intellectual flexibility. It is entirely understandable that this speech follows the conventions of Greek thinking, however, Barr presents this reference as if it substantiates his argument that Paul's Greek thinking applies to virtually all of the New Testament. Barr then extrapolates that understanding to imply that the Hebrew language is not relevant to understanding deeper meanings of Scripture. Barr's conclusion is simply not warranted from the evidence of this speech. (145) A closer look at just how much Paul explicitly aligns himself with Hebrew thinking is undertaken in chapter 13.

10.3 James Barr's Arguments.

Barr believes the linguistic evidence stands against the proposition that language contains implicit metaphysics. When Barr's five key arguments are examined it can be seen they point to specifically chosen and somewhat unique examples. We can agree with Barr's proposition that these examples show no clear link between the language and worldview in themselves, however, whether or not they justify Barr's conclusions is another question.

Greek thinking was fundamental to the development of logic. Logical thinking tells us that, because a relationship doesn't exist in a single instance it is not reason enough to prove that it cannot exist in another. To extrapolate from a single example to make a statement about every example is making a statement that is beyond the evidence. Barr is making assumptions that are beyond what can be logically inferred. This is what James Barr does when he claims that in the totality of the Hebrew language, there are no words that provide keys to understanding a Hebrew worldview. In this, Barr steps beyond the evidence. Chapter 11 of this book explores the possibility of developing an understanding of the Bible based on a study of Hebrew. In the estimation of this book, this understanding is both significant and meaningful. In chapter 11 there are examples of Hebrew words that, at the very least, disprove some of Barr's claims. In addition, there are examples of English and Greek words, without a Hebrew equivalent. The possibility of significant cultural understanding is explored.

A detailed and rigorous academic examination of each of Barr's arguments does not serve the purpose of this book. This book is written as a guide to help people explore the meaning of Scripture. The desired end result is that it will increase the reader's level of spirituality and intimacy with God. Chapter 11 of this book examines the Hebrew language and Hebrew thinking. Then it will provide examples of where Hebrew thinking brings significantly different perspectives than the Greek language and thinking. Barr's argument stands and falls on the quality of the evidence he provides. For those who are interested in a more detailed critique of James Barr's five key proofs, I recommend the analysis that can be found in Philip King's doctoral thesis turned into a book (2010) *Surrounded by Bitterness* (146).

Barr objects to the proposition that Hebrew thought, as represented by the Hebrew language, provides unique insights into the way we look at the world. Barr looks at the meanings of a range of Hebrew words and argues that there is no difficulty in translating these words into Greek or any other language. For Barr, the translation between Hebrew and Greek is sufficient to communicate the meaning of the text. For Barr, there is little theological value in examining the Hebrew text separately from the Greek translation.

Throughout his analysis, Barr focuses his arguments around the linguistic evidence and he acknowledges that there may well be differences in the worldviews of the Greek and Hebrew cultures, these differences, he argues, cannot be traced to the vocabulary or the grammar of the language. Barr's key argument is that this transition from language to the thought world of a culture is not possible. Barr is effectively rejecting the Whorf-Sapir hypothesis that language mirrors culture. It is the connection between culture and language that he argues against.

Specifically, Barr argues that the contrasts between Greek thought and Hebrew thought are far less radical than claimed and there are sufficient overlaps to make this distinction useful in any theological study. He rejects the idea that Hebrew is "unique," that the Hebrew "mind" can be understood from linguistic structures, or that there is a necessary correspondence between grammar and thought forms. Barr also denies that an understanding of the psychological elements of a culture can be determined by the culture's language.

Skip Moen is a popular Christian author with a Doctor of Philosophy from Oxford University. He writes that we can easily see the differences between Greek and Hebrew cultures when we look at the writings of the Old Testament. (147) His opinion is similar to that of many Jewish thinkers and theologians who argue that the Judaic interpretation of reality stands in marked contrast to the Greek view. This difference can be seen in multiple theological issues, which include sovereignty, justice, social structure, law, teleology and history. In each of these areas, Jewish thought is significantly different to Greek thought. In addition, the Jewish approach to exegesis, methodology, historical priority and theology is clearly different from the Greek approach. One significant area of difference is the way that the Greek approach embraces systematic theology. Systematic theology is entirely foreign to Hebraic thinking.

Barr may be correct in some of his linguistic analyses, however, his arguments cannot explain away these significant philosophical differences between the Hebrew and Greek cultures. Barr's principal objection is he denies that words, or phrases, in isolation can be an inadequate means of determining cultural perspective. Barr argues that the real meanings associated with language occur at a minimum at the sentence level, and perhaps at much larger slices of written and spoken material. Even if we grant Barr these criticisms (and we can even acknowledge that he disproves some claims of the Whorf-Sapir application to theological words), this is only a criticism of an inadequate methodology. Barr has not disproved the idea that language expresses reality from the perspective of the speaker. For instance, supporters of soccer and gridiron may use the terms playing field, goals, ball and referee, yet the meaning of these identical words changes in the different sporting contexts. (148) It should be noted that this perspective can be encapsulated in the understanding of single words without the need for entire sentences. For example, the word football is defined differently in different contexts.

Barr does present examples where meaning is not found in the word alone. Yet, Skip Moen argues that words from different cultures are like Venn diagrams that overlap. Some of the meaning is identical, but meaning can vary in different contexts. When we examine both the language and the culture, it is quite possible that ideas can differ markedly without the words themselves meaning something substantially different.

Barr's key criticisms are aimed at earlier research which assumed that language and vocabulary differences explained everything. What is interesting is the way the academic world has interpreted his understanding. This is discussed below. (149)

10.4 The impact of James Barr's thinking

In 2010, Philip King wrote about Barr's ideas and described how Barr's poor arguments have been critically applied to Sapir-Whorf style linguistics and have dominated the academic landscape for fifty years. (150) Hugh G. Williamson wrote Barr's obituary in the Guardian newspaper on November 8, 2006. it described Barr as " one of those few academics to whom it is given to write a book that changes the way a whole discipline is pursued. The fact that the discipline was biblical theology and that the book was only the first of many brings the scale of his achievements into even sharper focus" (151) Further, Williamson writes that Barr exposes the false belief that a culture's mentality can be understood directly from their language.

Academic writing about Barr is close to unanimous in recognising the significance of his impact. Barr's primary target is the argument within biblical studies that there are profound differences between Hebrew and Greek minds. The end result was that biblical studies became biased against any biblical analysis that pointed to the difference between Hebrew and Greek both in language and thinking. (152)

As we have read, much of Barr's writing was the use of examples that were correct in their specific context but those examples didn't prove the broader generalisations that have been applied to them. They certainly don't prove that every Hebrew word study of Scripture will be of no consequence. Jan Joosten, was also a Regus professor of Hebrew at Oxford University, (2014 to 2020). Joosten wrote about some of the limitations of Barr's work. He wrote that the implication that Hebrew thought could not be distinct from Greek thought was simply wrong. The Hebrew Bible contains many ideas that find a scant analogy in the Greek world and vice versa. Moreover, there can be no doubt that biblical notions are typically expressed in Hebrew. What is at issue is how strong the link is between language and biblical understanding, or in other words, to what extent can biblical ideas only be expressed in Hebrew? How much does an idea change if it is expressed in another language? More specifically, Joosten asks if the translation of the Hebrew Scriptures into the Greek language altered their Theology. These are questions that Barr does not answer clearly (153). Barr may have found examples where the connection between language and thought has been proven to be incorrect, however, this is far from proof that the connection never exists.

Joosten also notes that the philosophy of structuralism underpinned Barr's arguments. Structuralism is a philosophical perspective that sees language as a system. Barr insisted that theologians need to follow modern linguistics, and from his perspective, this means assuming that any analysis of language should view it as a system and avoid the examination of isolated parts or individual words. This means Barr was philosophically opposed to seeing individual words as significant. (154)

Joosten summarises his analysis of Barr by saying that as significant as Barr's contribution was to biblical studies, it must be remembered that his major contribution was in the field of criticism. Barr specialised in highlighting problematic reasoning and showing examples where translations were unable to achieve what they claimed, however, in terms of providing positive strategies for how biblical interpretation could be improved, Barr was largely silent. This is certainly true of his major work, *The Semantics of Biblical Language*. Joosten looks at Barr's criticisms and hopes that "Far from discouraging us from probing the relationship between language and thought they should spur us on to explore this issue further."(155)

This summarises a profound and far-reaching problem. The academic environment has largely embraced Barr's thinking and rejected any alternative. This has discouraged the analysis of the Hebrew language and the underlying philosophical issues it raises. In effect, the academic study of the Hebrew language has been suppressed, and along with it so has the potential that Hebrew thinking has to provide insights into the meaning of Scripture.

From an idealistic perspective, science is nothing but searching the evidence in order to find the truth. This perspective says the aim of academic thinking should be to follow the evidence wherever it leads. Alternatively, James Barr's critique comes with philosophical values and presuppositions that have suppressed insights that the Hebrew language can provide. Yet, as we will see in Chapter 11, the evidence shows that both the Hebrew language and Hebrew thinking can provide insights into biblical conceptualisation and meaning.

10.5 Can Bible scholars use Greek-style Thinking?

One of the most fundamental ideas in Greek philosophy is Aristotle's syllogism, where a conclusion is drawn from two preceding statements.

For example:

1. Socrates is a man.

2. All men are mortal.

Therefore, Socrates is mortal.

The truth is, it would be impractical for us to manage all of our technological devices without Greek thinking. It would also be impossible to write this book with its critical analysis without Greek thinking.

It is quite possible for a person to be spiritual and know God, yet need to think in a Greek way to solve a natural problem. The logic of deduction has helped us to develop our society in numerous ways. Logical thinking underpins all scientific experimentation and studies, especially in medicine and engineering. I believe that science and Christianity are entirely compatible. Greek thinking has its place in research and analysis. There is a key point of difference between Greek and Hebrew thinking. This key difference is that Greek thinking seeks to find answers from the human intellect whereas Hebrew thinking seeks to find answers from the human spirit and the presence of God.

Paul's argument for Hebrew thinking is largely encapsulated in 1 Corinthians 2: 13-14.

13 These things we also speak, not in words which man's wisdom teaches but which the Holy Spirit teaches, comparing spiritual things with spiritual. 14 But the natural man does not receive the things of the Spirit of God, for they are foolishness to him; nor can he know them, because they are spiritually discerned. NKJV

The key issue here is the priority of listening to the voice of God in a spiritual way occurs when believers seek to understand spiritual things. The Bible itself is making the clear statement that we cannot understand the Spirit of God with our natural intellect. The uncritical acceptance of Greek thinking in the halls of Christian theology violates this clear principle. This uncritical acceptance of Greek thinking has not just influenced Christian schools of Theology and Bible Colleges, this thinking has been the bedrock of theological training.

But this is not a universal statement. The Bible is not saying that Greek thinking is never a valid way to look at problems you encounter in your life. Once you establish the spiritual principle it can be perfectly appropriate to think about it in a Greek way. Greek thinking is largely evidence-based. It is not wrong for example to look at a group of people and say that if the average meal is $20 a head, then we will need $200 to feed ten people. This is evidence-based and logical. The inability to get a direct revelation from God in prayer about whether you have enough cash to pay for the meal is not an excuse, It's just wrong to say "I am avoiding Greek thought so how can I know if I have enough money to pay for this meal? All budgeting for example requires some level of Greek thought. This is an entirely different issue from saying " Does God want me to pay for this meal?" In fact, all budgeting issues can involve a tension between what you are currently capable of achieving which is Greek thinking, and the plans God has for your life which involves Hebrew thinking. To logically evaluate what something will actually cost is not wrong. The moral question about whether or not you should spend that money is a spiritual question which requires Hebrew thought,

The understanding that needs spiritual thinking is when we think about the things of God. This does not mean that the use of logical deduction never has a place once the important principles of God are established. But, there is a clear delineation. When churches present the things of God by using Greek-style intellectual analysis, this is a clear violation of this Scripture.

I am not saying there is no spiritual discernment in the Christian church, yet the focus of most contemporary church services is the presentation of ideas and intellectualisation. This is opposed to a relationship with God and spiritual transformation. 1 Corinthians 2: 13-14 speaks of things that are spiritual and this raises the question of where does the influence of spiritual things begin and end? Our modern life requires each person to make thousands of decisions each day. It is hard to imagine people asking God to help them with every single decision. Imagine, if at every intersection people would stop and pray before proceeding. This might make the world a spiritual place, but you would want to avoid city traffic, that is for sure.

Unless we base our relationship with God on a spiritual foundation we are in clear violation of biblical principles. We do not achieve this with a simple list of rules. This book argues that the reason so little thought is based on listening to God spiritually and being in a relationship with God has been the almost universal influence of Greek thinking. Greek thinking has been normalised and is thought of as an acceptable way to approach our faith. This book seeks to challenge Greek thinking as an acceptable way to approach faith. This is just the beginning of starting to live our lives in the intimacy that pleases God.

Chapter Eleven

Hebrew Language Insights

T his book has been examining the history of Greek thinking and how it has influenced the church. The academic
institutions of this modern western world, are based on Greek
philosophy and thinking. Greek thinking has provided the model
for the mindset of the western world and this mindset defines the
way most modern people view the world. The influence of Greek
thinking is so pervasive that those who live in our modern culture
are typically unaware of its influence. Greek thinking brings with it
a complete mindset that puts a priority on academic thinking and
the values of Greek philosophy. John Cleese, the famous comedian,
has written about the contrast between Hebrew and Greek thinking. He wrote, "It was a tremendous help to me to discover a few
years ago Aldous Huxley's description of the two different ways
in which we can approach religion. He speaks first of 'the religion
of immediate experience' A religion, in the words of Genesis, of
"hearing the voice of God walking in the garden in the cool of

the day", the religion of direct acquaintance with the divine. It sends shivers, doesn't it? Then Huxley contrasts this with... "the religion of symbols, the religion of the imposition of order and meaning upon the world through systems and their manipulation; the religion of knowledge about the divine, rather than direct acquaintance with it." (156) (157) It was previously mentioned that a key difference between the Greek and Hebrew mindsets is that in the entire Hebrew lexicon there is no word for mind. Hebrew people require no word that describes the mind and this is significant. Those of us with an English-speaking background can look at the English Old Testament and see that the word mind appears there. This can be simply explained as the original words that are translated as mind are heart H3280 and spirit H7307. (158) What we as Western thinkers have as our concept of mind could be better expressed from a Hebrew perspective as spiritual understanding. An understanding that comes from listening to God. The Hebrew focus is the search to understand what God is saying. This is opposite to the Greek focus, which is on developing your own understanding. (159) The Hebrew word for knowledge is also used to express a marital relationship. It is also used to describe the relationship between God and human beings. (Ps 16:11; Jer 9:23-24; Hos 8.2). From the Greek perspective, "knowing" means observation and analysis. Alternatively, the Hebrew concept of "knowing" is often expressed in terms of a walk with someone (Ps 95:10). The Hebrew concept of knowledge implies that there has been a commitment made to the person or the object to be known. Many of the teams that go out to preach the gospels on the streets are very caring and generous people. That notwithstanding, I do believe that identifying and eliminating the elements of Greek thinking in their interactions with people will help them to be more effective. Greek thinking brings philosophy and rhetoric. This approach leads people to focus on ideas. When speaking to people about their salvation the typical current strategy is to ask potential believers to say the sinners' prayer. It goes something like this: "Lord Jesus, I'm a sinner. I believe You died for my sins so I could be forgiven. I confess You are my Lord and Saviour. Thank You for coming into my life. Amen." The cause of the fall is outlined in Genesis 3:5. In 1993 Jacques B, Doukhan published a book called *Hebrew for Theologians*. Doukhan writes that Hebrew thought is at the very heart of the Old Testament. Hebrew thought also has significant implications for any understanding of the New Testament. According to Doukhan the very concept of thought in the Hebrew language is not the same as the Greek understanding of thought. In some ways to describe Hebrew thinking as thought is inaccurate. (160)The concrete metaphors of Hebrew thinking communicate emotion. The academic analysis of Greek thought is based on the language of detachment. Lois Tverberg in her book Reading the Bible with Rabbi Jesus says, "The goal of a logical proof is to convince hearers through facts and reason alone, without appealing to emotions. The Greeks valued detachment, subduing emotions so that intellect could reign supreme. But Middle Easterners believed it was just as important to convey the emotional component of their ideas." (161) From a Greek perspective emotional detachment is an important part of developing intellectual truth. The Greek approach values detachment so that the intellect can develop understanding without being distracted by emotions.

11.1 Overview General.

The Greek approach argues that our mind is the source of all knowledge, whereas the Hebrew approach says that God is the source of all knowledge. Greek philosophy embraces many Greek philosophers, each with their own emphases. The purpose of this book is to discuss the influence of Greek thinking on the church. The church father who did most to bring Greek thinking into the church was Augustine, and Plato was the Greek philosopher who influenced Augustine most. One of the main implications of Platonic thought is the idea that the physical/material world is evil and is separate from the world of ideas, which Plato considers good.

11.2 Overview 2 - Ways of approaching God.

The distinction that Cleese makes is incredibly profound as it identifies the core difference between Hebrew Thinking and Greek Thinking. This is a difference that permeates every aspect of these two approaches to God. The Greek approach is a system of knowledge that starts with humans asking questions to determine what they believe. The alternative Hebrew approach seeks to experience God and to discover what God would say to them. The Hebrew approach explores the possibilities of a relationship with God. Alternatively, Greeks describe God as distant and believe it is impossible for the God of purity to interact with this sinful world. Anyone who has been educated in the ways of the western educational system finds a natural bias towards approaching God in a Greek/analytical way. Alternatively, to think Hebraically, we will develop our understanding of God in a relational way.

In summary, if we seek to approach God like a Hebrew thinker, we must explore issues of intimacy and relationship with God and leave behind the intellectualisation of religion that comes with Greek thinking.

11.3 No Hebrew Word for Mind.

This kind of understanding makes sense in the context of 1 Corinthians 2:14.

1 Corinthians 2:14 But the natural man does not receive the things of the Spirit of God, for they are foolishness to him; nor can he know them, because they are spiritually discerned. NKJV

The Amplified Bible provides added nuance and explains it like this.

1 Co 2:14 But the natural, nonspiritual man does not accept or welcome or admit into his heart the gifts and teachings and revelations of the Spirit of God, for they are folly (meaningless nonsense) to him; and he is incapable of knowing them [of progressively recognising, understanding, and becoming better acquainted with them] because they are spiritually discerned and estimated and appreciated. AMP

This verse makes the significant point that the things of God are spiritually discerned. As God is Spirit this connection makes sense. This is clearly different from the natural mind or the Greek thinking approach which seeks to decide what is true by its own understanding. The Greek mind finds its fulfilment in knowledge which is a combination of what you understand personally and the thoughts of others that you agree with. When it comes to thinking about God this would typically be some kind of systematic theology. Paul refers to the natural man which in context is man's natural way of understanding. This contrasts with the Hebrew way of understanding, which is the way of seeking what God will reveal to you.

A Greek-style understanding seeks to read Bible commentaries and benefit from the wisdom of scholars. The Hebrew understanding of God comes from reading the Bible alone and praying for revelation. The implications of this verse are far-reaching. We can understand this verse as a comparison between Greek and Hebrew thinking. This verse is saying that the only way we can understand the Spirit of God is with our spiritual discernment. This concept of spiritual discernment is central to Hebrew thinking, yet the theological approach to understanding God is via intellectualism. This is the approach of Greek thinking, and they are very different.

11.4 Hebrew Knowledge comes from a Relationship.

With Greek thought, the ability to judge or make critical statements comes from someone who is observing externally and making decisions themselves. In Hebrew thought the ability to receive is implied. In Hebrew thought the true seat of one's intelligence is found in the ears. (Isaiah 50:5; Job 12:11). The Hebrew idea of intelligence means the ability to listen and to be open to the experience which comes before understanding. The biblical concept of intelligence is something to be received externally, intelligence is something better understood as a revelation.

This Hebrew emphasis on the ability to listen explains the importance of silence in Hebrew thought. For example, the Hebrew phrase that is translated as the still small voice literally means " the voice of a thin silence." (162) This comes from 1 Kings 19:12.

12 and after the earthquake a fire, but the Lord was not in the fire and after the fire a still small voice. NKJV

I recently came across a rarely quoted group of verses where Jesus is explaining an error of the Pharisees. In particular, there is verse 38 which says the Pharisees believe the Scriptures give them eternal life. The Pharisees are trying to highlight the ideas and laws in the Scriptures but Jesus explains the key to the Scriptures is himself. Salvation is not a matter of ideas even Scriptural ones, it is a relationship with Jesus.

John 5:37-40.

37 And the Father Himself, who sent Me, has testified of Me. You have neither heard His voice at any time nor seen His form. 38 But you do not have His word abiding in you, because whom He sent, Him you do not believe. 39 You search the Scriptures, for in them you think you have eternal life; and these are they which testify of Me. 40 But you are not willing to come to Me that you may have life. NKJV

The Greek style of thinking always looks to ideas, whereas Jesus focused on relationships, specific relationships with himself. This is because learning about God is not supposed to be a primarily mental activity. Here the Pharisees were searching the Scriptures, yet they were unwilling to come to Jesus so they could have life. The problem of the Pharisees is that they trusted in their intellectual approach even though they didn't have a relationship with Jesus. We must be careful not to follow their example.

11.5 The Hebrew priority is relationship.

The problem is that there are many who have prayed that prayer without changing their lifestyle. Often I have seen people pray that prayer when asked to by evangelists on the street, however, many are not seen again. The meaning of confessing Jesus as Lord is that you agree to obey Jesus in everything. Most people without a Christian background would not understand the concept of Lordship unless it was explained to them. In my experience, no explanation is given and the recipient of the prayer walks away without really understanding the words being spoken.

Despite what are typically good intentions, the sinner's prayer differs from the teaching of Jesus. In John 3:3, Jesus was asked, "How can a man be born again?"

John 3:5 Jesus answered, "Most assuredly, I say to you unless one is born of water and the Spirit, he cannot enter the kingdom of God. 6 That which is born of the flesh is flesh, and that which is born of the Spirit is spirit. 7 Do not marvel that I said to you, 'You must be born again.' 8 The wind blows where it wishes, and you hear the sound of it, but cannot tell where it comes from and where it goes. So is everyone who is born of the Spirit."NKJV

Again we have a contrast between the approach of Jesus who focuses on relationships and a spiritual connection as the key to salvation. This is different from approaches that accept a statement of orthodoxy as all that is required. This is a statement from the mind that may not have touched the heart or spirit, which is the key to Hebrew understanding.

The importance of the Holy Spirit is also seen In Ephesians 1:13, where the presence of the Holy Spirit within us is the proof of our salvation.

Ephesians 1:13 In Him you also trusted, after you heard the word of truth, the gospel of your salvation; in whom also, having believed, you were sealed with the Holy Spirit of promise. NKJV

In my experience, few unsaved people understand the implications of the words of the salvation prayer they are repeating as they are typically not explained. This approach is very consistent with the idea that the words themselves have some special powers. This idea that thinking and words are the keys to salvation originated in the Gnostic heresy (which comes from Greek thought). Gnostic is the Greek word for knowledge. Part of the Gnostic belief system is that secret words are all that is required for salvation. Jesus, however, focuses on being born again, which requires receiving the Holy Spirit. For Jesus, people are only saved if they are in a relationship with the Father, Son and Holy Spirit. Again, the Hebrew priority for relationship is in contrast to the Greek focus on words and intellect.

It is understandable that given the Greek origins of our education systems, our culture has the tendency to focus on ideas rather than relationships. When we apply the words and priorities of Jesus, salvation cannot be found in statements of orthodoxy, rather, it is found in relationships, especially spiritual connections. This connection comes with repenting and moving from the ways of the kingdom of darkness. It means moving away from a fleshy lifestyle and receiving the Holy Spirit within. This is the seal or proof of our covenant relationship with God. It is a mistake to think words of orthodoxy alone can establish that relationship.

John 5:37-40 was quoted in the previous section on relationships and is just as applicable to this section on salvation. By any measure, this verse is Jesus highlighting the importance of relationships and the focus on Him as the path to salvation. In the same few verses, Jesus criticises those who look at the Scriptures from the perspective of intellectualism. Jesus is saying the overriding objective of Scripture is to lead people into a relationship with him. This is the error of the Pharisees. In particular, verse 38 says the Pharisees believe the Scriptures will give them eternal life. The Pharisees are trying to highlight the ideas and laws in the Scriptures, but Jesus explains the overriding value is himself. Salvation is not a matter of ideas, even Scriptural ones find their true value in relationships.

John 5:37-40.

37 And the Father Himself, who sent Me, has testified of Me. You have neither heard His voice at any time nor seen His form. 38 But you do not have His word abiding in you, because whom He sent, Him you do not believe. 39 You search the Scriptures, for in them you think you have eternal life; and these are they which testify of Me. 40 But you are not willing to come to Me that you may have life. NKJV

As an overview, we can say, the Greek style of thinking always looks at ideas whereas Jesus focused on relationships. Learning about God is not supposed to be primarily a mental activity, it is supposed to be relational. The Pharisees are an example of people who search the Scriptures for years but end up with no personal relationship with Jesus. The problem of the Pharisees is that they trusted in their intellectual approach and ended up without a relationship with Jesus. We must be careful not to follow their example.

11.6 The Concept of Intentions compared to Actions.

In Hebrew, the verbs to hear and to do are synonymous. The Hebrew word for obedience is "shama". It means to hear, listen, give attention, understand, submit to, as well as to obey. So to hear and obey are the same word. The Hebrew word here is stressing physical action. This compares with Greek and Western culture where the stress is on mental activity. (163) This principle helps us understand Israel's response when they received God's laws. "We shall do, then we shall obey," (Exod 24:7).

The Hebrew version of Exodus 24:7 actually reads, "All that God had said we will do and we will hear." Again the link between hearing and doing is clear. Similarly, there is no Hebrew word that is equivalent to intentions. (164) Whereas, Greek-style thinkers embrace the word intentions. If we have good intentions it means we have good thoughts but there have been no actions. The Greek idea is that good thought somehow excuses the lack of activity and obedience.

The Hebrew mind understands that what God says must be done and people are evaluated not on what they say but on what they do. Alternatively, the Greek thinking approach evaluates thoughts instead of actions. The way of our culture is that obedience is optional, however, this is not the Biblical perspective.

11.7 The Fall

Genesis 3:5 For God knows that on the day you eat from it your eyes will be opened [that is, you will have greater awareness], and you will be like God, knowing [the difference between] good and evil." AMP

This verse makes a clear link between types of thinking and sin. What is this link? Most people understand that disobedience to God will always be sin, but how knowledge could be considered sin is a topic that is a topic that is rarely addressed. The fall was the transition between direct spiritual revelation from God to humans developing an understanding with our own understanding. The transition from our dependence on God in the Garden to making ourselves the deciders of what is good and evil. We have come to depend on ourselves and our understanding in order to determine what is good and correct, instead of asking God. It is the move from depending on God to independence. It is ultimately this quest for independent thinking that is responsible for the fall. Similarly, if we can develop an attitude of dependence on God, then to some extent God takes us back to the garden and reverses the damage of the fall.

11.8   Response to an Event

Hebrew thinking does not construct truth as a philosophical system. In fact, the irony of the book you are reading is that it seeks to present an argument that limits the usage of Greek thought. The only way to achieve this is by using the logical constructs of Greek thought, but what I am arguing for is based on the knowledge that has been gained from intimacy with God and Hebrew thinking. But let us leave that for a minute. (165)

According to *Hebrew for Theologians*, it is argued that Hebrew thought is essentially a response to an event. I would extend that to say Hebrew thought is typically the response to a relationship or an experience. In Hebrew, it is the thought that follows the event and not the reverse. In the Hebrew language words are normally derived from the verb, which shows the action coming before participants are aware of it. This idea that events come before they are understood is the way events happen and are taught in Scripture. (166)

The Creation event of Genesis chapter 1 follows this pattern. Here, history begins with an event in which human thought is totally absent. The human race becomes involved later. Similarly, salvation and the New covenant arrived prior to humanity being aware of the fact. The day of Pentecost also arrives with the briefest of explanations in Acts 1:8. (167)

Acts 1:8 is Jesus speaking to the apostles.

Acts 1:8: But you shall receive power when the Holy Spirit has come upon you, and you shall be witnesses to Me in Jerusalem, and in all Judea and Samaria, and to the end of the earth." NKJV

This is the briefest of explanations. There is no detailed explanation of the purpose and significance of the event. The pattern of Hebrew learning and knowledge comes through experience and walking with God. This pattern keeps repeating itself. The Greek approach of detailed tuition and notes occurring before an event just doesn't happen in the Bible. In the style of Hebrew thought the spiritual process involves a spiritual event which is followed by a response. Instead of thinking about the cause which led to the event as modern western thinking tends to do, ancient Hebrew thinking moves from effect to cause.

The Hebrew perspective is not a history interpreted from the perspective of thought and philosophical analysis. In the Hebrew mind, understanding comes from experience. If we look at an educational perspective, the Hebrew mind learns from the completion of a task, not the preparation for a task. In the next section, where we examine how the teaching of Jesus follows the Hebrew thinking model. Jesus gives brief instructions that provide experiences that lead to learning. Jesus avoids deductively explaining the logic behind events prior to people experiencing them.

11.9 Intellect vs Emotions.

In contrast, the Hebrew approach believes it is just as important to develop the emotional component of ideas. The Hebrew mindset values emotions. Crying and feelings are all healthy for the human condition. We are supposed to be full of love, peace and joy and there is an emotional component to each of these. The suppressed rigid person denies the reality of God's love.

It is true that sometimes God touches people, and they fall down and react. It is also true that when people are touched by God and freed from addictions strange things can happen. In Matthew 8:28-34 when Jesus delivered the demon-possessed man, those demons went into pigs, which then ran into the sea. The devil says bad things and wants to do bad things. Confronting him isn't always pleasant. But, the long-term results of being free are always good. The spirit of peace comes. If you are thinking from a Godly perspective, you will want these things gone. When you complain about the unpleasantness of what happens, the question to ask is who benefits from us not addressing the demonic?

Spiritual influences can make people react in strange ways, both good and bad. However, from a Hebrew perspective, emotions are nothing to fear. The problem comes when we pretend to be something we are not. The fruit of the spirit is love, peace and joy.

These are emotional. Being emotional is part of our humanity. Alternatively, the suppression of unpleasant ideas is anything but healthy for us.

The Bible is full of emotional characters like Paul, Peter, David, and Jesus. God loves positive emotions and it would be good if we can all embrace that.

Chapter Twelve

The Thinking and Preaching of Jesus

L ois Tverberg is a Jewish writer who has written about the teaching style of Jesus. Her book, (2017) *Reading the Bible with Rabbi Jesus* discusses the preaching topics of Jesus and how they include experience with knowledge of the natural world, Scriptures and human behaviour. (168) Doukhan, and his 1993 book *Hebrew for Theologians,* wrote that Hebrew thought is essentially a response to an event and, as was discussed in the previous section, that event is often a relationship or an experience. (169)

In 1897 Ernest D. Burton. wrote the article *Jesus As a Thinker* (170). Burton was a theologian and the president of Chicago University. This study about the way Jesus thought reveals just how different his thinking was from the typical Greek thought perspective of today. In this article, Burton writes about the unique style of Jesus' thinking and I have paraphrased some of his insights. Ralph and Gregg Lewis lectured in homiletics and in their 1989 book *Learning to Preach like Jesus* they identify the differences between the preaching of Jesus and most preachers of today. The most important difference is the contrast between the Inductive and deductive styles of preaching. Jesus preached in an inductive style, yet most of today's preachers prefer the deductive style which resembles the Greek style of thought. Alternatively, inductive preaching is like the Hebrew style of thought. (171)

In this chapter, the first discussion is about the way Jesus adopted the principles of Hebrew thought in his life and his preaching. The contrast between the approach of Jesus and the dominant values of Greek thinking is examined. *The Master Preacher* (1910) a book by A.R. Bond discusses the preaching style of Jesus. In it, Bond speaks of both the subjects that Jesus preaches as well as his communication methods. Jesus did not make his preaching intellectual. He made profound statements and achieved this by using simple words that communicated with his audience. Jesus avoided the intellectualism of Greek-style preaching. (172)

Jesus often aroused the emotions of his hearers. Amazement is recorded on 34 occasions. There is also anger, joy and hatred. Some of today's preachers create a message of shallow sensationalism as they seek to move their listeners. (173) Jesus was not like that. "Jesus came that men might know the truth, which is an intellectual process; that they might love God and men, which is an emotional process." (174)

12.1 Learning is a response to an event or experience

As Jesus calls the disciples it can be seen how closely his request follows Hebrew thinking. Let us read his call to discipleship in Matthew 4:18-22.

18 And Jesus, walking by the Sea of Galilee, saw two brothers, Simon called Peter, and Andrew his brother, casting a net into the sea; for they were fishermen. 19 Then He said to them, "Follow Me, and I will make you fishers of men." 20 They immediately left their nets and followed Him. 21 Going on from there, He saw two other brothers, James the son of Zebedee, and John his brother, in the boat with Zebedee their father, mending their nets. He called them, 22 and immediately they left the boat and their father and followed Him. NKJV

Jesus' request in Matthew 4:19 was "Follow me". The details of The Amplified Bible bring out the relationship aspect as the more detailed Amplified comments state that the disciples are invited to accept Jesus as their Master and Teacher, as well as walk the same path in life as he does. Even though the Amplified version mentions the concept of teaching this is not the teaching of Greek academic learning. This is the Hebrew style of teaching by example and relationship.

Matt 4:19 And He said to them, "Follow Me [as My disciples, accepting Me as your Master and Teacher and walking the same path of life that I walk], and I will make you fishers of men." AMP

These Amplified verses are interesting in that they explicitly describe the Hebrew process of teaching which focuses on relationships and sharing a walk with your teacher. When we look back to Adam in the Garden of Eden, the way our Heavenly Father taught was by walking in the Garden.

Genesis 3:8-11: And they heard the sound of the LORD God walking in the garden in the cool [afternoon breeze] of the day, so the man and his wife hid and kept themselves hidden from the presence of the LORD God among the trees of the garden. 9 But the LORD God called to Adam, and said to him, "Where are you?" 10 He said, "I heard the sound of You [walking] in the garden, and I was afraid because I was naked; so I hid myself." 11 God said, "Who told you that you were naked? Have you eaten [fruit] from the tree of which I commanded you not to eat?" AMP

It should be mentioned that the academic style of Greek style teaching is very different to the teaching style of Jesus, yet Greek-style training is typically what is provided for ministry students today. The other noteworthy element of these verses is Jesus' choice of the men that were being prepared to communicate the Christian faith to the world. They were predominantly engaged in physical work and not especially skilled in rhetoric or public speaking. The one exception in terms of physical work was Matthew the tax Collector. Jesus was engaged in physical work as a carpenter, this is certainly not academic work. However, ministry students of today are typically chosen because of their academic aptitude.

Notice that the request Jesus made to the disciples was " go and do..." The priority according to this request of Jesus was the activity component of his request, there was no mention of developing their academic skills so they could understand the task. Similarly, there were no detailed instructions, 10-point summary or lesson plan. There were no statements that justified or even explained the request. The approach of Jesus assumed that learning would come through relationships which is exactly the way Hebrew learning is shared.

An American psychologist, David A. Kolb has developed a model for learning known as *Kolb's experiential learning styles model*. This model is based on learning through experience. A UK company called Growth Engineering develops online learning based on Kolb's model. According to the Growth Engineering website, they have earned more than 110 awards for their learning products since 2013. (175) According to their website, Kolb's, " unique perspective on learning has had a big influence on the educational sector. In fact, research has that his theory is still the most commonly cited source in relation to reflective learning." (176)

The Hebrew approach to learning may be unconventional to some, however, contemporary research confirms that it is a very effective approach. There has been much research and one 2017 study was by Daniel J. Grady entitled *A Critical Review of the Application of Kolb's Experiential Learning Theory Applied Through the use of Computer Based Simulations Within Virtual Environments 2000-2016.* (177) In this study Grady has concluded that" It can be said that this theoretical foundation shows much promise in its future application within the area of virtual environments" (178) What this effectively means is that the experiential approach to learning is far from an antiquated idea. This experiential approach has been used by multiple researchers in the field of education and has helped them create solutions to contemporary commercial problems. Research is finding that students learn better from creating and experiencing rather than thinking theoretically.

12.2 Relationship and Jesus' Teaching

12.2.1 The woman caught in adultery.

The woman caught in adultery is one example of how Jesus counselled people brought before him. His words were notably brief. Let us read the encounter. After establishing that she had been caught in adultery, Jesus continues this way:

John 8:7-11 So when they continued asking Him, He raised Himself up and said to them, "He who is without sin among you, let him throw a stone at her first." 8 And again He stooped down and wrote on the ground. 9 Then those who heard it, being convicted by their conscience, went out one by one, beginning with the oldest even to the last. And Jesus was left alone, and the woman standing in the midst. 10 When Jesus had raised Himself up and saw no one but the woman, He said to her, "Woman, where are those accusers of yours? Has no one condemned you?"

11 She said, "No one, Lord."

And Jesus said to her, "Neither do I condemn you; go and sin no more."NKJV

After establishing what happened, the only advice Jesus gives this woman is to go and sin no more. There is no reasoning or moralising about the dangers of what she had done, just a very brief directive statement. For those of us coming from a Greek mindset, it would seem like she is being sent out into the world unprepared.

For the Hebrew perspective which underpins Jesus' approach, this simple word is enough. It is enough because these words are the beginning of a learning experience based on relationships. Spoken so that they are her key focus, as she plans her life in the future. The other thing that happens in this exchange is that she has been freed from condemnation as Jesus assures her that God does not condemn her in the way the religious crowd did. This was a life experience that we presume led to an increase in faith and the ability to perceive the world in a more faith-filled way.

12.2.2 The woman with the issue of blood.

Mark 5:25-34 25 Now a certain woman had a flow of blood for twelve years, 26 and had suffered many things from many physicians. She had spent all that she had and was no better, but rather grew worse. 27 When she heard about Jesus, she came behind Him in the crowd and touched His garment. 28 For she said, "If only I may touch His clothes, I shall be made well." 29 Immediately the fountain of her blood dried up, and she felt in her body that she was healed of the affliction. 30 And Jesus, immediately knowing in Himself that power had gone out of Him, turned around in the crowd and said, "Who touched My clothes?" 31 But His disciples said to Him, "You see the multitude thronging You, and You say, 'Who touched Me?'"32 And He looked around to see her who had done this thing. 33 But the woman, fearing and trembling, knowing what had happened to her, came and fell down before Him and told Him the whole truth. 34 And He said to her, "Daughter, your faith has made you well. Go in peace, and be healed of your affliction." NKJV

It is interesting that Jesus is the source of all truth, yet, he listens to the whole story from the woman and there is no mention of

Him saying anything as He does. In addition, Jesus refrains from taking the opportunity to launch into a detailed lesson. The first is that according to Jewish ceremonial law, having a woman with an issue of blood touch him should have left Jesus defiled. Jesus is silent on this matter as well as why he does not condemn her for her action. Secondly, there is the concept of faith. Jesus explains she is healed because of her faith but that is all he says about it. Jesus provides no explanation why it is important to "go in peace" or how she can "be whole of this affliction". In our Greek education systems, people crave further explanations of much of what Jesus said. They want to understand why Jesus ignored the Hebrew laws on cleanliness and why he specifically rewarded this act of faith. For Jesus, all that is required are very simple statements that reinforce the importance of our relationship with God. When Jesus spoke, his consistent priority was that believers should focus on their level of faith and in doing that develop their relationship with God. Yet these statements that Jesus made about faith are assumed to offer advice that is self-evident and there is no further explanation required.

Firstly, Jesus calls her Daughter emphasizing the level of intimacy her faith has brought her. The second statement of Jesus is especially interesting. Jesus says " Go in peace, and be healed of your affliction". This implies she makes the choice of whether she remains healthy or not. This is a directional statement that given our knowledge of the Hebrew learning process can be interpreted this way. Jesus is saying that she should seek to walk in the status of daughter which is the way he describes her and she should focus on going in peace. This can be seen as giving her a challenge that initiates a new level of her ongoing process of learning and healing.

This is the Hebrew way. The learning comes after the event and the teaching is very brief.

Jesus consistently either commends or rewards people for their faith, sometimes both. Here are some examples:

Matthew 8:10-13. When Jesus heard it, He marvelled, and said to those who followed, "Assuredly, I say to you, I have not found such great faith, not even in Israel! 11 And I say to you that many will come from east and west, and sit down with Abraham, Isaac, and Jacob in the kingdom of heaven. 12 But the sons of the kingdom will be cast out into outer darkness. There will be weeping and gnashing of teeth." 13 Then Jesus said to the centurion, "Go your way; and as you have believed, so let it be done for you." And his servant was healed that same hour. NKJV.

Matthew 9(29-30) Then He touched their eyes, saying, "according to your faith let it be to you." 30 And their eyes were opened. And Jesus sternly warned them, saying, "See that no one knows it." NKJV.

Matthew 15:28 28 Then Jesus answered and said to her, "O woman, great is your faith! Let it be to you as you desire." And her daughter was healed from that very hour. NKJV

Then we can read about his discussions when he deals with people for their lack of faith:

Matthew 6:28-34 28 "So why do you worry about clothing? Consider the lilies of the field, how they grow: they neither toil nor spin; 29 and yet I say to you that even Solomon in all his glory was not arrayed like one of these. 30 Now if God so clothes the grass of the field, which today is, and tomorrow is thrown into the oven, will He not much more clothe you, O you of little faith? 31 "Therefore do not worry, saying, 'What shall we eat?' or

'What shall we drink?' or 'What shall we wear?' 32 For after all these things the Gentiles seek. For your Heavenly Father knows that you need all these things. 33 But seek first the kingdom of God and His righteousness, and all these things shall be added to you. 34 Therefore do not worry about tomorrow, for tomorrow will worry about its own things. Sufficient for the day is its own trouble. NKJV

Matthew 8:26 But He said to them, "Why are you fearful, O you of little faith?" Then He arose and rebuked the winds and the sea, and there was a great calm. NKJV

Matthew 14:29-32 29 So He said, "Come." And when Peter had come down out of the boat, he walked on the water to go to Jesus. 30 But when he saw that the wind was boisterous, he was afraid; and beginning to sink he cried out, saying, "Lord, save me!" 31 And immediately Jesus stretched out His hand and caught him, and said to him, "O you of little faith, why did you doubt?" 32 And when they got into the boat, the wind ceased. NKJV

In each of these situations, the teaching of Jesus is very limited. Where he does teach, he takes things back to an example, typically, an example in nature such as the lilies of the field in Matthew 6:28-34.

The key principles of Hebrew thinking are in evidence. Firstly, Jesus avoids lengthy teaching and preparing people through education. Instead, Jesus provides simple directions such as Go your way; and as you have believed, so let it be done for you." Alternatively, there are simple corrections such as do not worry about tomorrow or why did you doubt? The assumption is that people will learn both from their walk with God after encouragement or correction. The other assumption is that detailed teaching is not required as the relationship will end up being a better teacher. This is after all the principle of Romans 8:14

14 For as many as are led by the Spirit of God, these are sons of God. NKJV.

12.4 Jesus and Salvation.

As our modern western culture is so dominated by Greek thinking it is common for modern Christians to focus on the intellect as the main path to God. Jesus himself speaks to the Pharisees about which of the intellect or relationship is the better path to prepare for salvation and Jesus tackles the issue head-on. The answer comes in John 5:37-40.

John 5:37-40. And the Father Himself, who sent Me, has testified of Me. You have neither heard His voice at any time nor seen His form. 38 But you do not have His word abiding in you, because whom He sent, Him you do not believe. 39 You search the Scriptures, for in them you think you have eternal life; and these are they which testify of Me. 40 But you are not willing to come to Me that you may have life. NKJV

The challenge that Jesus gives the Pharisees comes in two ways. The first challenge is his statement that "they have neither heard the voice of the Father or seen his form" and the second is that "you do not have the Father's words abiding within you". For a group of religious scholars who prided themselves on their ability to know God, this would have been shocking. The reason for all of this is "whom he sent, Him you do not believe" Effectively Jesus is saying that because they cannot recognise His relationship with our Heavenly Father the Pharisees cannot have the word abiding in them.

Because the Pharisees do not understand the relationship Jesus has with our Heavenly Father this leads them to have an inadequate understanding of who the Father is. We know this Scripturally because "whoever has seen me has seen the Father" (Matthew 14:9). The Pharisees focused on the intellectual elements of the scriptures, and they ignored or avoided the fact that the scriptures point towards a relationship with Jesus. This proves their understanding of the word is inadequate. In Jesus' words, this meant the word does not abide within them. In 1 Corinthians 2:12-14, Paul makes distinctions between different kinds of learning and I believe this is exactly what Jesus is referring to.

1 Corinthians 2:12-14 Now we did not receive the spirit of the world, but we received the Spirit that is from God so that we can know all that God has [freely] given us. 13 And we speak about these things, not with words taught us by human wisdom but with words taught us by the Spirit. And so we explain spiritual truths ·to spiritual people [or to those who have the Spirit; or with the Spirit's words]. 14 A ·person who does not have the Spirit [or natural person] does not accept the ·truths [L things] that come from the Spirit of God. That person thinks they are foolish and cannot understand them, because they can only be ·judged to be true [discerned; assessed] by the Spirit. NKJV.

To clarify Paul's statement, he is arguing that there are two types of wisdom: the spirit of the world and the Spirit of God. Without the Spirit of God, our understanding can only come from human wisdom. A naturally minded person does not accept truths revealed by the Spirit of God. In effect, spiritual thinking can only be understood by people who have the Spirit of God within them. This scripture is saying that people who have a relationship with the Spirit of God are able to understand spiritual things in a way that people without that relationship cannot. Similarly, people who rely on their natural minds cannot understand the Spirit of God.

The second part of the John 5 reference says

39 You search the Scriptures, for in them you think you have eternal life; and these are they which testify of Me. 40 But you are not willing to come to Me that you may have life. NKJV

As was established in 1 Corinthians 2:12-14, searching the scriptures is something that can be done by either the spiritual mind or the natural mind. If we interpret Greek thought as the natural mind, we could restate the scripture something like this.

"You search the scriptures looking for intellectual truth that will lead to salvation. The purpose of these scriptures is to testify of Jesus and help people to develop a relationship with Him.

The Greek concept of thinking correctly is juxtaposed against the Hebrew concept of correct relationship. Jesus is very consistent in his focus. In John 5 it is believing the words leading to a relationship with Jesus as opposed to thinking that ideas can bring salvation in themselves.

When we look back on the history of the church we can see the movement toward Greek thought developed over history. As a consequence, there are many sections of the church that focus on academic orthodoxy and/or orthodox confessions. These elements become the bedrock of their faith. The Ideas and the intellectual approach that go with them have dominated the church. This thinking is like that of the Pharisees. They sought salvation through Scriptures and ideas rather than their relationship with Him. Yet this is exactly why Jesus rebuked them. In most churches in the western world, the weekly focus is on sermons and the dissemination of ideas. This is in contrast to the example of Jesus with His consistent focus on the relationship with Him. In the next section, we will read his famous discussion with Nicodemus about salvation and see how Jesus describes his priorities in that discussion.

12.4.2 Salvation and Greek thinking.

Before I start this section I want to preface it by saying that I understand many of the teams that go out to preach the gospels on the streets are very caring and generous people. Leaving that to one side, I do believe that identifying and eliminating the elements of Greek thinking involved in street evangelism means evangelism will become more effective especially when the objective is to develop born-again relationships rather than obtain confessions of orthodoxy. The verse that is often referenced as a justification for the sinner's prayer is Romans 10:9-10:

9 that if you confess with your mouth the Lord Jesus and believe in your heart that God has raised Him from the dead, you will be saved. 10 For with the heart one believes unto righteousness, and with the mouth, confession is made unto salvation. NKJV.

The sinner's prayer is based on these verses and below I quote a popular version of it. The sinner's payer according to Questio nsGod.com is "if you declare with your mouth, "Jesus is Lord," and believe in your heart that God raised him from the dead, you will be saved. For it is with your heart that you believe receive justification. It is with your mouth that you profess your faith and are saved." (179) However, when we read the Amplified version there are some nuances not mentioned in other versions that are important.

Romans 9-10:9 because if you acknowledge and confess with your mouth that Jesus is Lord [recognizing His power, authority, and majesty as God], and believe in your heart that God raised Him from the dead, you will be saved. 10 For with the heart a person believes [in Christ as Savior] resulting in his justification [that is, being made righteous—being freed of the guilt of sin and made acceptable to God]; and with the mouth he acknowledges and confesses [his faith openly], resulting in and confirming [his] salvation. AMP

The Amplified version specifies that there needs to be an understanding that Jesus needs to be recognised as the one with power, authority and majesty. This is part of recognising that Jesus is Lord. The word Lord is not understood by many in today's society as when we confess Jesus is Lord we are giving Him the right to control our lives. The confession is a confirmation of what is in the heart. But when we are simply saying the words "we confess Jesus as Lord" and we do not understand them we are a long way from having the heart belief required for the biblical definition of salvation.

Jesus also made a statement in John 3:3 that "you must be born again". It is again setting a standard that is not met by a verbal confession of the sinner's prayer. A statement of intellectual orthodoxy is a long way short of the heart relationship that is required for salvation. Again our cultural bias teaches us that correct ideas are a way to salvation whereas the biblical standards are about the heart and relationship.

The problem is that there are many who have prayed the sinner's prayer without it changing their lifestyle. Many times I have seen people pray that prayer on the street with evangelists but they are never seen in church or at any event they are asked to attend. The meaning of confessing Jesus as Lord is actually agreeing to obey Jesus in everything. Most people without a Christian background would not understand the concept of Lordship unless it was explained to them. In my experience, no explanation is given and the recipient of the prayer walks away without really understanding the significance of what they have said. Certainly, they have not made the commitment that is ideal. Despite what are typically good intentions, the sinner's prayer is not what Jesus taught. In John 3:3, Jesus was asked "how can a man be born again?" Jesus answered the question in John 3:5.

Jesus answered, "Most assuredly, I say to you unless one is born of water and the Spirit, he cannot enter the kingdom of God. 6 That which is born of the flesh is flesh, and that which is born of the Spirit is spirit. 7 Do not marvel that I said to you, 'You must be born again.' 8 The wind blows where it wishes, and you hear the sound of it, but cannot tell where it comes from and where it goes. So is everyone who is born of the Spirit."NKJV

Again we have a contrast between the approach of Jesus who focuses on the relationship with himself. For Jesus in this instance relationship is a spiritual connection and that is the key to salvation. The sinner's prayer hopes these words or at least a statement of orthodoxy is all that is required. That statement may have been confessed but unless it touches the heart or the spirit that relationship connection is not there.

The importance of the Holy Spirit is also seen in Ephesians 1:13, where the presence of the Holy Spirit within us is the proof of our salvation. Ephesians 1:13 In Him you also trusted, after you heard the word of truth, the gospel of your salvation; in whom also, having believed, you were sealed with the Holy Spirit of promise NKJV

In my experience, few unsaved people understand the implications of the words of the sinner's prayer they are repeating as it typically goes unexplained. This approach is very consistent with the idea that the words themselves have some special powers. The idea that thinking and words are the keys to salvation originated in the Gnostic heresy (which comes from Greek thought). Gnostic is the Greek word for knowledge and part of their belief system was that secret words are the key to salvation. Jesus, however, focuses on being born again which entails receiving the Holy Spirit. For Jesus people are only saved if they are in a relationship with the Father, Son and Holy Spirit. Again the Hebrew priority for relationship is in contrast to the Greek focus on words and intellect.

12.4.3 Jesus and Salvation / Doctrine v fruit.

The Amplified version of Matthew 7:15 -20 provides another insight into this issue of salvation and the importance of adopting a Hebrew perspective. It reads:

Matthew 7:15 -20 "Beware of the false prophets, [teachers] who come to you dressed as sheep [appearing gentle and innocent], but inwardly are ravenous wolves. 16 By their fruit you will recognize them [that is, by their contrived doctrine and self-focus]. Do people pick grapes from thorn bushes or figs from thistles? 17 Even so, every healthy tree bears good fruit, but the unhealthy tree bears bad fruit. 18 A good tree cannot bear bad fruit, nor can a bad tree bear good fruit. 19 Every tree that does not bear good fruit is cut down and thrown into the fire. 20 Therefore, by their fruit you will recognize them [as false prophets]. AMP

In summary, this verse is saying we can test a person's relationship with God by a person's behaviour or fruit. This is based on Galatians 5:19-25.

19 Now the practices of the sinful nature are clearly evident: they are sexual immorality, impurity, sensuality (total irresponsibility, lack of self-control), 20 idolatry, sorcery, hostility, strife, jealousy, fits of anger, disputes, dissensions, factions [that promote heresies] 21 envy, drunkenness, riotous behaviour, and other things like these. I warn you beforehand, just as I did previously, that those who practice such things will not inherit the kingdom of God. 22 But the fruit of the Spirit [the result of His presence within us] is love [unselfish concern for others], joy, [inner] peace, patience [not the ability to wait, but how we act while waiting], kindness, goodness, faithfulness, 23 gentleness, self-control. Against such things, there is no law. 24 And those who belong to Christ Jesus have crucified the sinful nature together with its passions and appetites. 25 If we [claim to] live by the [Holy] Spirit, we must also walk by the Spirit [with personal integrity, godly character, and moral courage--our conduct empowered by the Holy Spirit]. AMP.

The fruit of the spirit is what comes when the Holy Spirit lives within us. This Scripture is saying it is important that our behaviour is consistent with the fruit of the spirit. The reason is that behaviour is what comes from the presence of the Holy Spirit within a person. Again it is the Hebrew standard of relationship that is biblical. There is no word for intentions and obedience is assumed.

12.5 Thinking like Jesus

12.5.1. Jesus never spoke about topics like philosophy or politics. Unlike other thinkers who comment on a diverse range of topics, Jesus confined himself to talking about our relationship with God and associated topics like spirituality and morality. His answers were worded in a simple and easy-to-understand manner.

12.5.2. For example when Pilate asked Jesus, "Are You the King of the Jews?" Jesus replied, "It is as you say." NKJV (Mark 15:2) Jesus never got involved in an academic style discussion and his unique thinking style was different from the Rabbis.

12.5.3. The rabbinic ideal of a scholar is someone who can receive exactly what has been taught and transmit it to others without change. This contrasts with the teachings of Jesus which came not from a mind full of the thoughts of others. Even when Jesus taught Old Testament principles he added his own unique perspective. (179) Jesus can be understood to be following the principles of Hebrew thinking and the Scriptures, yet he reinterpreted them in his own authoritative way. In addition, Jesus directed his followers in the paths of the new covenant as no one else could. Despite the breadth of his teaching, he never provided anything but brief answers. In short, Jesus never provided academic answers to the questions he faced. Jesus was extremely independent in his thinking. He quotes extensively and approvingly from the Old

Testament, yet he asserts his superiority over it. Jesus makes himself the final authority.

12.5.4. Jesus did not engage in philosophical argument and his thought consistently communicated the Hebrew idea that we need to seek God spiritually. The first part of this is getting our relationship right.

12.5.5. In the words of Burton, "The thinking of Jesus was penetrative and germinal "(180) as opposed to thinking systematically. This means that Jesus communicated ideas that were relevant and important, rather than a detailed system of ideas that could be thought of as philosophical analysis.

12.5.6 Burton classifies great thinkers into two categories. One is poetic or prophetic the other is organizing or scholastic. The first category makes powerful observations that speak for themselves while the second builds systems of thought. Burton places Jesus in the first category as " a prophet..not a system-maker, but a thinker, a seer".(179) As Burton describes the preaching mission of Jesus, "he was concerned to tell men about God, not the infinite and the absolute but the Heavenly Father ". (180) What Burton is saying is that the preaching of Jesus did not present the God of philosophical debate or theological analysis. Instead, Jesus spoke of our Heavenly Father i.e. the God who is personal and cares for his children. When Jesus spoke he almost universally spoke about the God of relationship, or how to live our lives on earth in a way that pleased our Heavenly Father. Jesus also prioritised the building of relationships with his hearers (181)

The thinking of Jesus was positive and constructive. He made statements like "All things are possible to those who believe". Jesus recognised people had choices and faith can change things.

Jesus consistently appealed to reality or what can be experienced and observed, as opposed to the theoretical and abstract. This is how Burton describes the preference Jesus had for using inductive rather than deductive logic. This is discussed in section 12.7.

12.6 Preaching like Jesus.

Parables are a key part of Jesus' preaching. The parables summarise complex messages and express them as a story. A western or Greek mindset summarises ideas in terms of concepts. Lois Tverberg provides the example of Isaiah 53:7 in her book *Sitting at the feet of Rabbi Jesus* (2017), where Jesus is compared to the lamb. (182)

Isaiah 53:7 He was oppressed and He was afflicted, Yet He did not open His mouth [to complain or defend Himself]; Like a lamb that is led to the slaughter, And like a sheep that is silent before her shearers, So He did not open His mouth. AMP

The concept is that "God's servant will suffer injustice". This reading of Isaiah is not just a concept of the lamb, there are added emotional connections. The innocence of the lamb who was slain. The silence of the lamb, who we know was well able to defend himself. This story has a heightened sense of injustice. When thought is reduced to an academic concept it is stripped of most of its emotional power and is examined in a detached way. Greek-style thinking brings with it the ideal of finding truth in its own emotionally detached way. When emotions are suppressed logic rules.

For Hebrews the inclusion of the emotional side of the argument is important. (183)

We can think in terms of the heart-rending messages of Scripture, the incredible sacrifices not just of Jesus but of many of the main figures, both of the Old and New Testaments. The heroes of the Bible are no strangers to emotion. The struggle Abraham had when God asked him to take Isaac to the place of sacrifice. The struggle Moses had with leadership, The struggle David had with his feelings for Bathsheba. Yet in the hands of Greek-style preaching, these great human examples of faith can be stripped of much of their passion and emotion. In the hands of those who promote this style of Greek thought, God is often seen as harsh and judgemental. How else can you explain the suffering that exists in the world that God controls? While many will try and paint a picture that there is some greater good being achieved, how does the mother of a child that has died from a fatal disease see the cause of that event as anything but cruel and unjust? These dimensions of Greek thought have alienated many from the love of our Heavenly Father. It is well overdue for the church, which claims to represent God, to stop perpetuating this cruel misrepresentation of our loving Heavenly Father.

From a Hebrew point of view, our Heavenly Father sacrificed His own son to save us, because he sees humans are valuable. This view of human beings is why his apostles were called to make great sacrifices so that the lost would be saved. In Scripture, we see how like a lamb led to slaughter Jesus put aside his spiritual authority in order to create a covenant that would break the curse of sin over all humanity. Is it possible to preach this message in a detached unemotional way?

12.6.2 Preaching like Jesus beyond Definition.

Karl Barth the famous German theologian said "No attempt is made in the Bible to define God—that is, to grasp God in our concepts. . . . The Bible tells the story of God; it narrates His deeds and the history of this God as it takes place on earth in the human sphere. The Bible proclaims the significance and the importance of this working and acting, this story of God, and in this way, it proves God's existence and describes His being and His nature. The Bible is not a philosophical book, but a history book, the book of God's mighty acts, in which God becomes knowable to us." (184)

The stories of history are presented by the prophets and writers of Scripture. The events where God encounters mankind are described. Our knowledge of God is limited by our understanding of multiple events. As Abraham Herschel has said "Speculation starts with concepts, biblical religion starts with events... To the Jewish mind, the understanding of God is not achieved by referring to the qualities of a supreme being, to ideas of goodness or perfection, but rather by sensing the living acts of His concern, to His dynamic attentiveness to man...God's goodness is not a cosmic force but a specific act of compassion. We do not know it as it is but as it happens." (185)

The Hebrew people do not try to reduce God to a definition; definitions place him in the same category as all the other false man-made gods of the nations who were made to satisfy their own desires and aspirations. Instead, the God of Israel stands alone limitless and unsearchable. Unlike the gods of the ancient world, The God of the Bible revealed Himself for relationship and was not simply there for their personal benefit. More than that the God of the Bible was" a Father, a Husband, a Protector...a PERSON...not merely an entity" (186). This was very different to the gods of the ancient world.

Part of this indefinable nature is seen when Moses stood in the presence of the burning bush and asked God his name in Exodus 3:14. (187)

14 And God said to Moses, "I AM WHO I AM." And He said, "Thus you shall say to the children of Israel, 'I AM has sent me to you.' "

What we do know is that the Christian faith came into existence through prophetic promises to Israel and the appearance of the Messiah Jesus. Understanding what happened requires us to interpret the words of scripture and to understand the events of History.

12.6.3 Greek Brain/ Hebrew Brain: The Way Parables Work.

Most of the time Jesus spoke about what could be experienced and this contrasted with the if-then logic of Greek deductive thinking. When Jesus explained his reasoning it was always based on experience rather than if-then logic. The most common way that Jesus taught about spiritual reality was to make comparisons with what could be observed in nature and daily life. Sometimes Jesus spoke about what is obviously true, for example, grapes don't grow on a thorn bush. Similarly, we can understand people by observing their "fruit."

Jesus also taught that nature teaches spiritual reality. The fact that a tiny mustard seed has the potential to grow into an enormous tree is the basis for one of Jesus' parables. Jesus taught us that our material world is complex. If God's creation is surprising then shouldn't our Creator surprise us too? In contrast, Western deductive reasoning typically attempts to help us understand God by making everything predictable and systematised.

Jesus also often used examples based on human experience in order to explain the complexity of God's ways. For example, if a farmer finds tares growing in his wheat fields, wouldn't it be best to pull them out? Knowing that the process of pulling the tares out would damage the valuable wheat crop, the farmer decides to let the tares grow. In the same way, God allows evildoers to live alongside the righteous. This is an example of Jesus answering the questions of philosophers through his storytelling.

What Jesus is saying is that which might seem illogical at first. The choices of a farmer match a parallel situation in which God must make a decision. Jesus reminds us that God knows the wider situation and for the overall good he delays harsh judgement. Jesus reminds us that what is seemingly illogical at first is not in God's greater wisdom. (188)

12.6.4 Themes of the Scriptures.

Parables often use themes and images from the Scriptures.

According to Bond's 1910 book, *The Master Preacher*, Jesus used seven key themes:

The Kingdom of God (This was the theme Jesus used most often. It was mentioned 78 times in the KJV)

God the Father

Eternal life

Self-denial

Sin and righteousness

Love

His death and resurrection (189)

These are topics of significance and as noted previously Jesus never spoke on philosophy, reform or politics. Jesus spoke so that His themes were almost universally connected to everything. Wherever possible Jesus sought to make people open to the presence and love of God, as well as to present mankind with their responsibilities. These are all images that appear in Jesus' parables as well as those of other rabbis. Both the plots and the punchlines could allude to scenes in the Bible.

12.7 Preaching like Jesus: Induction v deduction

In their analysis of preaching Lewis and Lewis, they have identified multiple factors that identify Jesus' preaching. They include:

It is personal and preaches to human need

Uses stories, parables and narrative logic.

Shares common experiences

Preaches with verbal pictures

Uses comparison and contrasts

Moves from specific instances to general concepts

Asks questions and then guides to concepts

Loves and respects his listeners more than his power

Says come unto me not agree with me (190)

12.8 Deductive or inductive preaching part 2

12.8.1 Deductive or left-brained preaching includes:
Theologians with propositions
Dogma
Abstractions
Theory
Reason
Proof
Left brain accent
Theologians assumed authority by preaching

12.8.2 Inductive or right-brained preaching includes:
Parables
Metaphors
Stories
Questions
References to experience
Life and examples
Achieves authority in preaching. (191)

The contrast between Hebrew and Greek thought is reflected in the contrast between inductive and deductive logic. The Stanford Encyclopaedia of philosophy states that "inductive logic is the logic of evidential support". (192) This means inductive logic comes to conclusions by observation and evidence. This contrasts with deductive logic where multiple ideas or logical propositions are presented in an academic way in order to argue for a specific conclusion. This is the way of academic argument. Logical deduction is the way of intellectualism that underpins much of Greek thinking.

In chapter 11 where we looked at Hebrew thought it can be seen that Hebrew thinking places a priority on what is observed and experienced, whereas the analytical approach of deduction comes from Greek-style thought and is foreign to a Hebrew understanding. The classic example of deductive logic is Aristotle's syllogism (193). This deductive style of thought often leads to the long and sophisticated arguments that are common in contemporary preaching. This is the style that dominates the homiletics courses of today. In the centuries starting around the 4th century BC, an oratory style of professional rhetoric or speech became very popular entertainment in the Greek-speaking world. In the church after the first century AD, the preaching of simple stories started to fade. The rhetorical and deductive style of preaching that dominates today's homiletics rose to popularity.

When we look at the previous chapter and its focus on relationships we can see how this fits into the simple preaching style of Jesus. Inductive preaching makes a priority of specific examples, especially personal testimonies. It is interesting that the word testimony occurs 76 times in the King James translation of the Bible. Clearly, the Bible values a personal story. These stories all follow the inductive tradition,

In summary, not only was the preaching style of Jesus personal it was simple and short. The priorities of Jesus can be better understood after our previous look at Hebrew thought. Not only is there a clear focus on relationships there is also a rejection of intellectualism. In addition, we can see the focus of Jesus on reality and examples of that reality. Jesus embraced the observational style of inductive thought and parables, rather than the intellectualism and abstract thinking of deductive thought. We can also see that rather than giving teaching in a theoretical way Jesus invited people to have experiences that encouraged their relationship with God.

Jesus' style of teaching and lesson content exemplified the Hebrew perspective. Without actually verbalising it, Jesus is rejecting all manifestations of Greek thinking. What should be obvious has not been understood by any but a minority of Christian believers. In John 14:9 Jesus said, "Whoever has seen me has seen the Father." This means is we want to communicate in a way that is consistent with the character of our Heavenly Father. A way that develops mutual understanding.

This means Hebrew thinking should be incredibly significant for anyone seeking to understand the God of the Bible. Here the example of Jesus is making the statement that the best way to communicate with our Father is to communicate in a personal and intimate way. This is a very significant understanding. An understanding that should be well understood by those who claim to represent Him.

Chapter Thirteen

Paul and Greek thinking

P aul was fluent in both Hebrew and Greek (as well as other languages), St. Paul was well aware of the difference between Greek and Hebrew thinking. The choice between Greek or Hebrew style thinking was not something Paul thought was irrelevant, nor was it a topic that Paul was silent about. Paul was an opinionated man and he expressed his beliefs clearly. Acts 18 verses 24-28 help us understand Apollos and his background. While Apollos may have been an articulate apologist for the early Christian faith until he met Priscilla and Aquila he was unaware of the baptism of Jesus, he only knew about the baptism of John. There is no culture or system of thought more strongly identified with worldly wisdom than that built around the Greek philosophers. The Amplified version of 1 Corinthians 1:20, as quoted below, has some very interesting aspects to it. For the sake of the argument let us call what is in brackets the definition of the original word, then the wise men are defined as philosophers, the scribes are defined as scholars and the debaters are defined as logicians and orators. At the time when Paul wrote this verse these definitions of philosopher, scholar, logician and orator all embody the intellectualism of Greek thinking.1 Corinthians 2 continues this theme that contrasts worldly wisdom and spirituality. The first 5 verses are very pointed in their contrast between Greek and Hebrew thinking. There is a contrast between the academic approach, and the Hebrew approach, to understanding Scripture. The Hebrew idea that understanding comes from our spirit (heart or soul) is very clearly alluded to in 1 Corinthians 2:14.What this Wesley Hills article above shows us is that many respected theologians have beliefs that are diametrically opposed to what could be described as the first century or Pauline biblical view. (194) Systematic theology leads to its focus on doctrinal questions such as Christology and the doctrine of the Trinity. This is according to thinkers like Karl Barth, whereas theologians such as Rudolph Bultmann also added the concept of demythologising and the removal of supernatural thinking. In addition, Greek thinking for which Diessmann shows a distinct preference makes its own impact, often that impact is the creation of a sense of superiority.

The way Hill and others reject the writings of Paul because they are not "theological" follows a familiar theme. Those that uncritically embrace Greek thought instead of Hebrew thought seem to develop a sense of superiority. It seems that much of the academic world has followed the lead of James Barr and essentially defined the study of Hebrew thought, as having little or nothing to offer, yet this belies the words of Scripture. These are the Scriptures that academic theology claims are only really understood with their help. When Paul's teaching gets presented to the world through the lens of Greek-style theology, the two chapters of 1 Corinthians 1 and 2 tend to be ignored. Yet here are almost two full chapters that in many ways represent foundational texts required to understand the writings of Paul. After all, Paul is saying in 1 Corinthians 2:4 that his ministry comes from a Hebrew perspective and in the next verse that this should be the foundation for our faith. I understand there are many people living in western cultures who have followed the teaching of the leaders of their denomination, and done this in an academic way. This promotes the idea it is possible to learn about God through studying commentaries and systematic theologies. In addition, it may be possible to understand things about God when preachers preach in a sophisticated manner. However, Paul's message is outspoken in his rejection of Greek thought.

13.1 The Teaching of 1 Corinthians 1.

Today's readers of the Bible face multiple hurdles before they can really understand the importance of what Paul is saying. The first is that our culture has been so indoctrinated by Greek thought and understanding that any objective analysis is extremely difficult and rarely discussed. The dominance of the Greek style of thought has been further enhanced by the success of the European Enlightenment. The importance of science in our society has brought an analytical and scientific perspective to life which in turn has brought with it significant technical advances and a generally improved quality of life. On the negative side, since the Enlightenment so-called scientific thinking has become more aggressive. The most aggressive forms of this thinking include scientific materialism and scientism, these worldviews deny any kind of spiritual reality and that means they deny the existence of God. There has been a significant shift in societal values. This is a rejection of spirituality that has influenced even those who believe in the existence of God. Many Christians have developed the belief that even though He exists, God operates from a distance and spiritual events are unusual. This is the view that N.T.Wright describes as Deism.(195)

It is not surprising then that Paul's critique of Greek thinking is going to be lost on the vast majority of those reading the Bible today. As is explained later in this section, Paul is very clear that he rejects Greek-style thinking and instead endorses a Hebrew-style understanding. This understanding of Paul's writing is an explicit endorsement of Hebrew thinking as it has been described in the previous two chapters of this book. Paul's argument supports the view that Greek thinking is in conflict with the original Hebrew understanding of the Bible and faith with Biblical values follows the pattern of Hebrew thinking. This is consistent with the premise of this book which says that Greek thinking has distorted the practice of the Christian faith to be unbiblical.

The letters of Corinthians were letters that Paul wrote to the relatively new church in the city of Corinth approximately 50 AD. (196) This is a city in Greece that was a centre of commerce. For Paul, the actions of Apollos and the presence of Greek thinking presented a potential threat to the growing church. In the early chapters of Paul's teachings, which are 1 Corinthians chapters 1 and 2, Paul makes his case against the Greek way of thinking.

In 1 Corinthians 1:12. Paul writes about the man Apollos. Apollos, a Jewish man with a Greek name was born in Alexandria Egypt. Alexandria was a city known for its library and the influence of Greek intellectualism. According to G.V. Lechler a 19th-century writer, "Apollos was indebted to the school of Philo both for his method of Scriptural interpretation and for his eloquence. But the Platonic character of Philo's school of Old Testament interpretation was so alien from anything that would have led to a humble reception of Christian truth, that we wonder at that excellent man and able critic making such a concession to the enemies of the truth; nor can we imagine Apollos to have almost anything in common with that school, except its rooted faith in the supernatural foundation of the Jewish Religion and the inspiration of the Scriptures, and a love of biblical interpretation." (197)

13.2 Apollos: Acts 18 (24-28).

Acts 18:24 Now a Jew named Apollos, a native of Alexandria, came to Ephesus. He was an eloquent and cultured man and well-versed in the [Hebrew] Scriptures. 25 This man had been instructed in the way of the Lord, and being spiritually impassioned, he was speaking and teaching accurately the things about Jesus, though he knew only the baptism of John; 26 and he began to speak boldly and fearlessly in the synagogue. But when Priscilla and Aquila heard him, they took him aside and explained more accurately to him the way of God [and the full story of the life of Christ]. 27 And when Apollos wanted to go across to Achaia (southern Greece), the brothers encouraged him and wrote to the disciples, [urging them] to welcome him gladly. When he arrived, he was a great help to those who, through grace, had believed and had followed Jesus as Lord and Savior, 28 for he powerfully refuted the Jews in public discussions, proving by the Scriptures that Jesus is the Christ (the Messiah, the Anointed). AMP

While Acts 19:1 to 6 specifically says that Paul and Apollos were in different cities, these verses talk of disciples who, like Apollos, had not received baptism in the name of Jesus. When these disciples received the baptism of Jesus they received the Holy Spirit. It is very reasonable to assume that Apollos received this baptism later, as well.

Act 19:1-6: 1 It happened that while Apollos was in Corinth, Paul went through the upper [inland] districts and came down to Ephesus, and found some disciples. 2 He asked them, "Did you receive the Holy Spirit when you believed [in Jesus as the Christ]?" And they said, "No, we have not even heard that there is a Holy Spirit." 3 And he asked, "Into what then were you baptized?" They said, "Into John's baptism." 4 Paul said, "John performed a baptism of repentance, continually telling the people to believe in Him who was coming after him, that is, [to confidently accept and joyfully believe] in Jesus [the Messiah and Savior]." 5 After hearing this, they were baptized [again, this time] in the name of the Lord Jesus. 6 And when Paul laid his hands on them, the Holy Spirit came on them, and they began speaking in [unknown] tongues (languages) and prophesying.

Apollos was an eloquent man, (Acts 18:24) some Corinthians preferred Apollos and his version of Christianity to that of Paul (1 Corinthians 1:12). In 1Corinthians 1:17 Paul confirms that he was a legitimate apostle, despite his lack of eloquence in comparison with Apollos. Further, Paul is saying that his lack of eloquence makes the cross more effective.

1Corinthians1:17 For Christ did not send me [as an apostle] to baptize, but [commissioned and empowered me] to preach the good news [of salvation]--not with clever and eloquent speech [as an orator], so that the cross of Christ would not be made ineffective [deprived of its saving power]. AMP

Paul's reference to Apollos as an eloquent man and presumably the better orator seems to confirm Lechler's contention that Apollos was taught by Philo. Philo sought to integrate the Hebrew scriptures into Greek philosophy. Philo believed in a transcendent God without any emotional qualities. All these features of Philo's teaching are typical of Greek thought, as they describe a distant unemotional God, who they seek to relate to in an intellectual and academic way. In verse 17, Paul is saying that men should not be persuaded to come into baptism because of human eloquence. Paul makes the statement that the power of the Cross can be made ineffective where salvation is preached with cleverness and eloquence. Just think about that for a minute. Typically, the desired standard of Western preaching, especially when it comes from an academic background, is to be eloquent. This polished professional educated style of delivery of the message of the cross is not what Paul is seeking to achieve. Paul expands on the theme in verse 18.

1Corinthians 1:18 For the message of the cross is foolishness [absurd and illogical] to those who are perishing and spiritually dead [because they reject it], but to us who are being saved [by God's grace] it is [the manifestation of] the power of God. 19

For it is written and forever remains written, "I WILL DESTROY THE WISDOM OF THE WISE [the philosophy of the philosophers], AND THE CLEVERNESS OF THE CLEVER [who do not know Me] I WILL NULLIFY." 20 Where is the wise man (philosopher)? Where is the scribe (scholar)? Where is the debater (logician, orator) of this age? Has God not exposed the foolishness of this world's wisdom? 21 For since the world through all its [earthly] wisdom failed to recognize God, God in His wisdom was well-pleased through the foolishness of the message preached [regarding salvation] to save those who believe [in Christ and welcome Him as Savior]. AMP

Paul argues that the Wisdom of God will destroy the wisdom of men as the two types of wisdom are absolutely incompatible. This claim of Paul's may be considered to be controversial however, it is absolutely consistent with other scriptures. This verse is entirely in line with Matthew 11:25, 1 Corinthians 3:18-19, and Isaiah 5:21.

Matthew 11:25 At that time Jesus said, "I praise You, Father, Lord of heaven and earth [I openly and joyfully acknowledge Your great wisdom], that You have hidden these things [these spiritual truths] from the wise and intelligent and revealed them to infants [to new believers, to those seeking God's will and purpose]. AMP

1Co 3:18 Let no one deceive himself. If anyone among you thinks that he is wise in this age, let him become a fool [discarding his worldly pretensions and acknowledging his lack of wisdom], so that he may become [truly] wise. 19 For the wisdom of this world is foolishness (absurdity, stupidity) before God; for it is written [in Scripture], "[He is] THE ONE WHO CATCHES THE WISE and CLEVER IN THEIR CRAFTINESS;" AMP

Isaiah 5:21 Woe (judgment is coming) to those who are wise in their own eyes and clever and shrewd in their own sight! AMP

Most Bible College homiletics courses seek to develop oratory excellence in their students, yet Paul is saying that this eloquence can make the cross ineffective. According to Paul, the cross is not a topic to be preached with eloquence. The cross is the place where humanity should come with an awareness of our need for the sacrifice of Jesus. The cross represents the Spirit and power of God and we should acknowledge the fact that the sacrifice of Jesus overcame the sin of the world. The way Paul makes this argument in the context of the division with those who support Apollos highlights a specific aspect of the argument. The argument is that there is a choice between the intellectual approach of the Greeks, as Philo taught Apollos or the contrasting approach of the spirituality and relationship-focused style of Hebrew thinking.

13.3 Greek Thought and Worldly Wisdom.

1 Corinthians 1:20 Where is the wise man (philosopher)? Where is the scribe (scholar)? Where is the debater (logician, orator) of this age? Has God not exposed the foolishness of this world's wisdom?

This verse links Greek intellectualism with the foolishness of the world's wisdom. This makes sense, especially in the context of Paul's discussion about Apollos and can be interpreted as a direct criticism of the pride and self-righteousness that comes from Greek-style thinking. When we adopt the Greek approach, which embraces the wisdom of the world, it fails to really understand the God who has come for the weak and the humble.

As Christians, we are not to trust in the intelligence of men but rather in the power of God. In 1 Corinthians 20, Paul states that human wisdom, as expressed in philosophy and debate, are both hallmarks of Greek thinking and are expressions of the wisdom of the world. As Christians, we are instead to embrace the cross and the God who has exposed the true foolishness of worldly thinking. In context, this worldly wisdom of foolishness comes packaged in Greek thought which ultimately fails to recognise God. Even when Greek thought is used to discuss God, it seeks to do so through the agency of human ability. The cross is a proclamation not of the ability of mankind but the need of mankind. If we come to the cross with a mind full of thoughts about humanity's abilities we miss the true message as the cross is the provision for the separation from God that initially exists in the human condition. As Paul is about to say in 1 Corinthians 2:4 He comes not in the wisdom of men but the power of God. Paul wants his church to know God in a relationship and to know God spiritually not intellectually.

What we can see in Paul's writing here are very explicit arguments against Greek thought which is a theme that he continues to the end of 1 Corinthians 2. First, there are the specific mentions of Greek thinking:

1 Corinthians. 1:22b The Greeks seek after wisdom

As a side note, the mention of Jews requiring a sign in 1 Corinthians 1:22a is a statement regarding the Jews who were controlled by the religious elite of the day. While it is not inconsistent with the Hebrew language and its desire for direct connection with

God, it is inconsistent with the way the Hebrew language values experience as a path to knowledge.

1 Corinthians 1:23 But we preach Christ crucified, unto the Jews a stumbling block, and unto the Greeks foolishness;

1 Corinthians 1:24 But unto them which are called, both Jews and Greeks, Christ the power of God, and the wisdom of God.

(As a side note there are also multiple references to Jews and Greeks in the book of Acts)

Acts 14:1 - ... a large number of Jews, as well as Greeks believed

Acts 18:4 - ... trying to persuade Jews and Greeks

Acts 19:10- ...Jews as well as Greeks

Acts 19:17- ...both Jews and Greeks

Acts 20:21- ...both Jews and Greeks

The Jews and Greeks represent the Jews and the Gentiles and their respective modes of thought. Jews represent those who are the inheritors of the biblical mindset whereas the Greeks represent the dominant language and culture of the world at that time. The contrast between Hebrew and Greek thought is a central part of the thesis of this book. What Paul is saying is the distinction between the two is essential for a biblical understanding. The following sections include an examination of the specific mentions of Greek thought in Corinthians. It is especially helpful to use the Amplified version which brings out a number of implied references.

1 Corinthians 1:23 but we preach Christ crucified, [a message which is] to Jews a stumbling block [that provokes their opposition], and to Gentiles foolishness [just utter nonsense], 24 but to those who are the called, both Jews and Greeks (Gentiles), Christ is the power of God and the wisdom of God. 25 [This is] because

the foolishness of God [is not foolishness at all and] is wiser than men [far beyond human comprehension], and the weakness of God is stronger than men [far beyond the limits of human effort]. 26 Just look at your own calling, believers; not many [of you were considered] wise according to human standards, not many powerful or influential, not many of high and noble birth. 27 But God has selected [for His purpose] the foolish things of the world to shame the wise [revealing their ignorance], and God has selected [for His purpose] the weak things of the world to shame the things which are strong [revealing their frailty]. 28 God has selected [for His purpose] the insignificant (base) things of the world and the things that are despised and treated with contempt, [even] the things that are nothing, so that He might reduce to nothing the things that are, 29 so that no one may [be able to] boast in the presence of God.30 But it is from Him that you are in Christ Jesus, who became to us wisdom from God [revealing His plan of salvation], and righteousness [making us acceptable to God], and sanctification [making us holy and setting us apart for God], and redemption [providing our ransom from the penalty for sin], 31 so then, as it is written [in Scripture], "HE WHO BOASTS and GLORIES, LET HIM BOAST and GLORY IN THE LORD." AMP

13.4 The Teaching of 1 Corinthians 2.

1Co 2:1 And when I came to you, brothers and sisters, proclaiming to you the testimony of God [concerning salvation through Christ], I did not come with superiority of speech or of wisdom [no lofty words of eloquence or of philosophy as a Greek orator might do];2 for I made the decision to know nothing [that is, to forego philosophical or theological discussions regarding inconsequential things and opinions while] among you except Jesus Christ, and Him crucified [and the meaning of His redemptive, substitutionary death and His resurrection]. 3 I came to you in [a state of] weakness and fear and great trembling. 4 And my message and my preaching were not in persuasive words of wisdom [using clever rhetoric], but [they were delivered] in demonstration of the [Holy] Spirit [operating through me] and of [His] power [stirring the minds of the listeners and persuading them], 5 so that your faith would not rest on the wisdom and rhetoric of men, but on the power of God. AMP

In Chapter 2 especially verses 4 and 5, the concept of power is emphasised. For Paul, the alternative to Greek-style wisdom is the presence of the power of the Holy Spirit. This power comes in two ways. First, there is the demonstration of the Holy Spirit through answers to prayer and second, there is the power of God stirring the minds of the listeners. This is very much the concept of spiritual understanding that comes from the spirit or heart as we discussed before in our conversation about the lack of the word mind in the Hebrew language.

In the more direct NKJV 1Corinthians 2:4read like this:

4 And my speech and my preaching were not with persuasive words of human wisdom, but in demonstration of the Spirit and of power, 5 that your faith should not be in the wisdom of men but in the power of God. NKJV

Here Paul is making a statement about the priorities of his ministry. Paul is making another explicit rejection of the intellectualism inherent in the Greek approach and stating this is not how he wants to represent his ministry. The word rhetoric refers to skills of public speaking and is found in the Amplified version. This is a clear reference to Greek thought. The famous Greek Philosopher Aristotle (384-322 BC) wrote a 3 volume work called "*The Art of Rhetoric*". Another Greek philosopher Quintilian (35-100 AD) wrote a book called "*Training of an Orator*". This is a book about rhetoric and is considered by many to be the most influential educational textbook ever written. (198) Paul is repeating his rejection of Greek intellectualism. For Paul, the correct alternative is to communicate the gospel message with a demonstration of spiritual authority. This power comes from a spiritual relationship with God and is a clear allusion to spiritual gifts. Paul writes more about the gifts later in Corinthians. Paul is not just saying that he chooses to focus on spiritual relationships rather than intellectualism, he is saying we should choose Hebrew thought over Greek thought.

For those readers who think my critique of Greek thought is too harsh, remember this, Paul was the man that the angel of light chose as the apostle to lead the evangelistic effort of the faith. Paul was one of the most educated men of his day and Acts 22:3 says that Paul was educated at the feet of Gamaliel. Gamaliel was the most notable Hebrew scholar of the day. Paul is not a man whose ideas can be easily dismissed.

Paul's credentials are beyond question and his words speak clearly against the cultural standards of today. If you seek to take the Bible seriously it is important to recognise what Paul is saying.

Paul continues in 1 Corinthians 2:6-7:

Yet we do speak wisdom among those spiritually mature [believers who have teachable hearts and a greater understanding]; but [it is a higher] wisdom not [the wisdom] of this present age nor of the rulers and leaders of this age, who are passing away;7 but we speak God's wisdom in a mystery, the wisdom once hidden [from man, but now revealed to us by God, that wisdom] which God predestined before the ages to our glory [to lift us into the glory of His presence]. AMP.

The purpose of this spiritual wisdom is to move us away from a natural understanding to be able to challenge the understanding of these hidden levels of spiritual wisdom. This higher level of spiritual truth is spoken of in 1 Corinthians 2:8-12.

1Co 2:8 None of the rulers of this age recognized and understood this wisdom; for if they had, they would not have crucified the Lord of glory; Co 2:9 but just as it is written [in Scripture], "THINGS WHICH THE EYE HAS NOT SEEN AND THE EAR HAS NOT HEARD, AND WHICH HAVE NOT ENTERED THE HEART OF MAN, ALL THAT GOD HAS PREPARED FOR THOSE WHO LOVE HIM [who hold Him in affectionate reverence, who obey Him, and who gratefully recognize the benefits that He has bestowed]." 10 For God has unveiled them and revealed them to us through the [Holy] Spirit; for the Spirit searches all things [diligently], even [sounding and measuring] the [profound] depths of God [the divine counsels and things far beyond human understanding]. 11 For what person knows the thoughts and motives of a man except the man's spirit within him? So also no one knows the thoughts of God except the Spirit of God. 12 Now we have received, not the spirit of the world, but the [Holy] Spirit who is from God, so that we may know and understand the [wonderful] things freely given to us by God.

In these verses, Paul discusses the need for Christians to be taught by the Holy Spirit and to avoid human wisdom. This raises two points. Firstly, this kind of knowledge is a challenge to the cultural understandings of today and second, the higher wisdom of God is not understood even by the rulers of this age. Through the Holy Spirit, we have access to the spiritual thoughts and knowledge which enable us to be guided. This guidance enables us to understand wonderful things. Here again, Paul is making a contrast between worldly knowledge and the things of God. He is also prioritizing the spiritual value of the teaching. These are powerful words. Then in 1 Corinthians 13-14, Paul says the things of God are understood by spiritual discernment.

1Co 2:13 We also speak of these things, not in words taught or supplied by human wisdom, but in those taught by the Spirit, combining and interpreting spiritual thoughts with spiritual words [for those being guided by the Holy Spirit]. 14 But the natural [unbelieving] man does not accept the things [the teachings and revelations] of the Spirit of God, for they are foolishness [absurd and illogical] to him; and he is incapable of understanding them because they are spiritually discerned and appreciated, [and he is unqualified to judge spiritual matters]. AMP

The simpler NKJV says it this way:

13 These things we also speak, not in words which man's wisdom teaches but which the Holy Spirit teaches, comparing spiritual things with spiritual. 14 But the natural man does not receive the things of the Spirit of God, for they are foolishness to him; nor can he know them, because they are spiritually discerned. NKJV

The point is again the need to contrast Greek thought, which is based on human wisdom, and Hebrew thinking which is based on spiritual discernment. The things of God can only be understood spiritually. To express it another way, it is impossible to understand the things of God when we approach them from the perspective of Greek intellectualism. To make the point even more clearly those who approach God from an academic perspective cannot understand the Spirit of God. There are many people who have invested years of their life into this Greek academic approach.

In 1 Corinthians 1:4-5, it reads

I thank my God always for you because of the grace of God which was given you in Christ Jesus, 5 so that in everything you were [exceedingly] enriched in Him, in all speech [empowered by the spiritual gifts] and in all knowledge [with insight into the faith]. AMP

According to the Jamieson Faussett Brown commentary on 1 Corinthians 1:5 (199), it was in their speech and knowledge that the Greek Corinthians were most proud of. Here Paul is reminding them that faith is understood by spiritual gifts and is a matter of grace given to them as gifts from our Heavenly Father. Later in the chapter, Paul writes about the demands of the Jews and the Greeks in 1 Corinthians 1:22 - 24:

For Jews demand signs (attesting miracles), and Greeks pursue [worldly] wisdom and philosophy, 23 but we preach Christ crucified, [a message which is] to Jews a stumbling block [that provokes their opposition], and to Gentiles foolishness [just utter nonsense], 24 but to those who are the called, both Jews and Greeks (Gentiles), Christ is the power of God and the wisdom of God. AMP

This Jewish demand for signs is a reflection of Jewish expectations of the time. At the time of Jesus, they were hoping for the appearance of the Messiah and the miraculous signs they were expecting that would confirm his appearance. The religious expectations of the Jews were largely directed by the Pharisees who did expect miracles.

As for the Greek world, their pursuit of wisdom and philosophy was well known and it is clearly stated in the Amplified version that the message of Jesus crucified is nonsense to the Greek mind. Whenever Greek thinking is mentioned, Paul places it in opposition to the things of God.

1 Corinthians 1:24 but to those who are called, both Jews and Greeks (Gentiles), Christ is the power of God and the wisdom of God. 25 [This is] because the foolishness of God [is not foolishness at all and] is wiser than men [far beyond human comprehension], and the weakness of God is stronger than men [far beyond the limits of human effort] 26 Just look at your own calling, believers; not many [of you were considered] wise according to human standards, not many powerful or influential, not many of high and noble birth. AMP

So for those Jews and Greeks who are called or who believe, things are different, Jesus is not seen as foolish but as the power of God. Jesus is not foolish at all despite what he appears to be to those who are unsaved. Verse 25 states that God is stronger than men which, while it may not be the only intention of this verse, the context would suggest it is written to expose the foolishness of Greek humanism and to be a challenge to those ideas.

The next verses are 1 Corinthians 1:26-31.

26 Just look at your own calling, believers; not many [of you were considered] wise according to human standards, not many powerful or influential, not many of high and noble birth.

27 But God has selected [for His purpose] the foolish things of the world to shame the wise [revealing their ignorance], and God has selected [for His purpose] the weak things of the world to shame the things which are strong [revealing their frailty].

28 God has selected [for His purpose] the insignificant (base) things of the world, and the things that are despised and treated with contempt, [even] the things that are nothing, so that He might reduce to nothing the things that are,

29 so that no one may [be able to] boast in the presence of God.

30 But it is from Him that you are in Christ Jesus, who became to us wisdom from God [revealing His plan of salvation], and righteousness [making us acceptable to God], and sanctification [making us holy and setting us apart for God], and redemption [providing our ransom from the penalty for sin],

31 so then, as it is written [in Scripture], "HE WHO BOASTS and GLORIES, LET HIM BOAST and GLORY IN THE LORD." [Jer 9:24]

13.5 The Academic Challenge to Paul

14 But the natural man does not receive the things of the Spirit of God, for they are foolishness to him; nor can he know them, because they are spiritually discerned. NKJV.

This verse is not an isolated statement but comes within the context of 1 Corinthians 2 where Paul clearly states a natural man without the Spirit of God, even a very intellectual man, cannot understand Spiritual things. The understanding of spiritual truth comes from our relationship with God. Mankind can not really know God when we approach Him from an intellectual or philosophical perspective. The second idea implied in this verse is that real spiritual understanding comes from the spiritual nature of our being.

As we have read, Paul describes his ministry in 1 Corinthians 2:4-5, yet theological thinking has come to be dominated by Augustine and the influence of Greek thinking. That thinking has caused Paul's statements to be re-interpreted as statements that support Greek thinking at the cost of Hebrew thinking. In the book of Acts revival was the property of all the church and could be understood by all who received God's Spirit. Yet, it has become accepted dogma since the 4th century that the message of Christianity is best understood when we study theology or approach things from the perspective of Greek thought. This is opposed to the Hebrew or experiential perspective of the day of Pentecost and the actual teachings of Jesus, St. Paul and the early church. The dominance of Greek thought amongst both the educated classes and the leadership of the church has meant that Greek thought has been largely unchallenged in the broader church: Catholic, Protestant, Reformed and Charismatic.

There are many academics who are dismissive of the academic skills of St. Paul. One of them is Wesley Hill. He is the author of a 2012 article, "St. Paul Theologian of The trinity"(200). Wesley is an American theologian who has examined the broader question of where Paul fits in the world of systematic theology. He writes, "It's become commonplace in modern literature on the Apostle

Paul to observe that he wasn't a systematic theologian. One need look no further than a standard textbook from the last century, which offers the colourful exhortation not to "rank the tent-maker of Tarsus along with Origen, Thomas Aquinas, and Schleiermacher." "Paul did not theoretically and connectedly develop his thoughts," adds Rudolf Bultmann, the titan of twentieth-century New Testament scholarship, "as a Greek philosopher or a modern theologian."(201) According to Wesley Hill, "Paul was a pastor, missionary, and letter-writer, not a member of the Sorbonne." (202)

Hill's initial point is that the contemporary evidence argues against seeing Paul as a systematic theologian. In making his point, Hill cites the writings of Adolph Diessmann (1866-1937) who was a prominent German protestant theologian. In 1912 Diessmann writes that Paul does not really belong to the world of theology and is better classified within the world of religion (203). For Diessmann "Paul belongs with the Herdsman of Tekoa and Tersteegen, the ribbon weaver of Mulheim". (204). To say that Diessmann has chosen these groups of people in a dismissive and condescending way is an absolute understatement. Diessmann argues that Paul is very limited in his vision. The most positive thing that Diessmann saw in Paul was that he was a hero of religion. To Diessmann and those like him, Paul's theology was secondary. To paraphrase Diessmann, Paul's naivete was more powerful than his capacity to reflect. His propensity to be mystical was stronger than his capacity to write dogma. Diessmann's argument continued when he said that Paul's relationship with Christ was more important to him than his Christology, and his relationship with God was more powerful than his capacity to write a doctrinal statement about

God. Diessmann concludes by saying that Paul was " far more a man of prayer, a witness, a confessor and a prophet, than a learned thinking exegete and a close thinking scholastic". (205)

Diessmann's condescending attitude and explanation show he is thinking from a Greek perspective and does not understand that Paul is writing from a Hebrew perspective, much less that Paul is differentiating between the Greek and Hebrew approaches to knowledge. What Diessmann has written could well be considered a compliment from the Hebrew perspective. For those seeking to be intimate with God, it is far more valuable to be taught by a man of prayer, than an analytical scholastic. Diessmann has, in his critical and academic way, recognised that Paul is presenting biblical truth from the experiential and relational perspective. However, to enlist Bultmann as a voice that would deny Paul the status of a theologian is simply wrong. The sentence that Hill quotes is accurate in itself, but it is far from an accurate summation of Bultmann's position. There is a more complete transcript of the original document that can be found in the references (206). After no more than two intervening sentences Bultmann says "These facts must not be allowed to lead one to a false conclusion that Paul was not a real theologian nor to the notion that to understand his individuality he must be regarded, instead, as a hero of piety. On the contrary! The way in which he reduces specific acute questions to a basic theological question, the way in which he reaches concrete decisions on the basis of fundamental theological considerations, shows that what he thinks and says grows out of his basic theological position—the position which is more or less completely set forth in Romans." (207)

When we read this more complete version of Bultmann's quote it can be seen that the original quote has been selectively copied in a way that hides the actual views of the author. Even the source document makes the specific statement that Hill's conclusion is false. (208) As academic as Greek thinking theologians may be, to assume that their ideas are always the result of unbiased and flawless research is clearly not true, this instance proves it. The assumption that some have unspoken agendas is indisputable.

What Hill, and some other critics of Paul, fail to appreciate, is that the intelligence behind the thought and language of Scripture has, with minor exceptions, chosen to present the biblical message from the Hebraic perspective. The challenge for intimacy and experience is central throughout Scripture. However, as Paul wrote so eloquently in 1 Corinthians 1:19. The God of Scripture seeks to destroy the wisdom of the wise and the cleverness of the clever.

N.T. Wright, a theologian, whom this book commends for his critical thinking, identifies this problem in his own eloquent way. He has identified that many who write systematic theology assume " that the Jewish setting can be set aside. Some theologians argue that because Paul taught justification by faith and not works he is teaching from a non-Jewish perspective." (209) N.T Wright continues shortly after to say in effect that the end result is that, "the study of Paul, in these highly influential movements at least, has partaken of what I perceive actually to be the problem afflicting so much systematic theology to the present day: the assumption that the Jewish setting of the original texts can and even must be set well aside in order to allow a non-Jewish discourse to proceed unchecked. To this, for the moment, I merely say one thing: that

at least in Paul's mind the idea of the worldwide mission was itself
a profoundly *Jewish* idea," (210)

Later in his article and book N.T. Wright says "My central proposal is that systematic theology would do well to try to give
twenty-first-century answers to first-century questions; and that
the first-century questions might themselves give us some clues as
to how to do that."(211) The first century was the time when the
apostles were still alive and Jewish thinking was still the standard.
The first century was before Platonic and Gnostic ideas began to
distort the church's understanding of the Bible.

I would add that the very intellectualism that comes packaged
with theological thought brings with it the distorting influence of
Greek philosophy, however, a true return to first-century thinking
removes the church from layers of Greek thinking and reveals the
Jewish heart of our Heavenly Father.

13.6 The spirituality of Paul vs Theology.

The presentation of St. Paul as a man of poor exegetical skills
and scholarship is unjust at a deep level. Here is a man who was a
scholar and had a superior level of understanding of both Greek
and Hebrew languages and thought. In Paul, we find a love of
spiritual gifts and prophecy that combines with his desire to bring
the God of intimacy and power to the people. His writings have
inspired many and it is my hope that Paul's understanding of the
need for the spirituality, that comes with Hebrew thinking, can
reinvigorate the church. The world is desperate for it. The world

needs a church that opens the door to true spiritual healing and the consequent spiritual empowerment it brings.

13.7 Paul and Power.

1 Corinthians 2:4-5: And my message and my preaching were not in persuasive words of wisdom [using clever rhetoric], but [they were delivered] in demonstration of the [Holy] Spirit [operating through me] and of [His] power [stirring the minds of the listeners and persuading them], 5 so that your faith would not rest on the wisdom and rhetoric of men but on the power of God. AMP

The fact that the Bible is saying we should base our faith on Hebrew thinking and not Greek thinking seems unavoidable. Not only is it the most obvious interpretation of this Scripture, but it is also the interpretation that best fits the context of 1 Corinthians 1 and 2. These chapters are full of criticism of Greek thought as well as the promotion of the Hebrew perspective. It seems unavoidable that Paul is teaching the church to reject Greek thinking as it relates to godliness and further he is arguing that this is essential for true spirituality.

What is to be done with these chapters? Reinterpret them? When we looked at Augustine and his presentation of a Greek thinking interpretation of Scripture it is understandable that those who support this understanding prefer these sections of Scripture to be ignored or at the very least re-interpreted. This results in a theological worldview that leads the church away from true spirituality and away from intimacy with our Heavenly Father.

In the days of Justin Martyr, the Hellenization of Scripture could be seen as a way to stop the suppression and oppression of the faith. (212`) It is quite plausible that Justin had good intentions as his stated reason for wanting Greek translations was so they would make the Scriptures more understandable to the academic elite and understood by speakers of the dominant language of the day. Those days have long passed, and we currently exist in a world that is largely alienated from God. In saying that, I believe this includes many people who have a desire to follow Him. Few have really understood the Hebrew approach and God's desire for intimacy. In the Western church, those who make a priority of having the Holy Spirit living within them seem to be in the minority. It is a concept that seems to be ignored by large parts of the Western church. The theology that justifies this approach brings with it a systematic misinterpretation of the words of Jesus, Paul and John.

What are we witnessing here? For some, it might be the world's incapacity to think clearly. For others, it might be a statement of the profound sinfulness of mankind. I believe it is the reality of a spiritual power that specifically opposes Christian spirituality. This is a reality that is more influential than seems to be recognised, a worldly spiritual power that wants mankind to focus on our own abilities and to think that God appreciates an intellectual presentation of His gospel. This power loves to keep people away from an intimate spiritual relationship with their Heavenly Father. We will read more about it when we discuss the writings of John the Apostle.

These Greek-style gospel interpretations were developed by a group of church leaders who felt good about keeping the gospel message distant. A message that conformed to the sensibilities of the Greek-speaking world. This message at its heart has produced a message without power. It is a message that kept people at arm's length from the spiritual embrace of God's kingdom. It is a message that has made people feel their statements of doctrinal orthodoxy were sufficient. Packaged with this message has come the clandestine rebirth of Gnosticism, bringing its promise of salvation through knowledge. This time not in the hands of a group of external heretics, but this time it has come in the hands of the church fathers who shaped the faith in the centuries that followed.

13.8 Hebrew thought is connected to spiritual power.

I believe there are two key reasons for Paul's argument. The first is that unless we have a spiritual connection then we cannot be born again. This is simply foundational to the faith according to Jesus in John 3:3. The spiritual connection comes as we seek the reality of a relationship with our Heavenly Father, not just seek to understand him. The alternative is setting ourselves up to be the judge, seeking to evaluate all. In this approach, at some level there is an unavoidable sense of self-righteousness as with it there is a pointing to one's own abilities and efforts. The Hebrew approach enables the Spirit of God to flow in your life. When we are justified by the blood of Jesus and embrace the manifest presence of God, we have nothing to prove.

The second reason for Paul's Hebrew thinking approach is alluded to in 1 Corinthians 2:4, here Paul says he comes in the power of God. We can combine this with an understanding of Ephesians 6:12. Let's look at the verse.

Ephesians 6:12 For we do not wrestle against flesh and blood, but against principalities, against powers, against the rulers of the darkness of this age, against spiritual hosts of wickedness in the heavenly places NKJV

Ephesians 6:12 is saying our battle is a spiritual battle, or that a spiritual battle is what Christians are called to. Spiritual battles can only be fought with spiritual weapons such as prayer, faith and the word of God. All parts of the armour of God as found in Ephesians 6:10 and 11.

Jesus asked his followers to seek first the kingdom of God in Matthew 6:33 and Matthew 6:9-13.

Mathew 6:33 But first and most importantly seek (aim at, strive after) His kingdom and His righteousness [His way of doing and being right--the attitude and character of God], and all these things will be given to you also. AMP The Kingdom of God is repeatedly the priority of Jesus and is included in the Lord's prayer of Matthew 6:9-13.

Matthew 6:9-13: In this manner, therefore, pray:

Our Father in heaven, Hallowed be Your name. 10 Your kingdom come. Your will be done on earth as *it is* in heaven.11 Give us this day our daily bread. 12 And forgive us our debts, As we forgive our debtors. 13 And do not lead us into temptation But deliver us from the evil one. For yours is the kingdom and the power and the glory forever. Amen. NKJV

Jesus wants us to always seek the Kingdom and in 1 Corinthians 4:18-20 Paul makes this very interesting statement:

1 Corinthians 4:18 Now some are puffed up, as though I were not coming to you. 19 But I will come to you shortly if the Lord wills, and I will know, not the word of those who are puffed up, but the power. 20 For the kingdom of God *is* not in word but in power. 21 What do you want? Shall I come to you with a rod, or in love and a spirit of gentleness? NKJV.

Again there is a contrast between the intellect and spiritual power. Paul wants to focus on the Kingdom of God which is based on spiritual power. The strong influences of both Greek thinking, and the Enlightenment means Paul's focus is not what is taught in most of today's churches. Instead, the gospel has in many ways been taught as a humanist and Deist caricature of the first-century gospel message.

The Christian church has typically embraced academic thinking, much of it dry and unemotional. Yet, the power of God is left untouched. Irrespective of the approach of much of the church, the Spirit of God is poised to transform all who genuinely seek that transformation. For Paul, the key to mature Christian faith is not the intellect but the level of spiritual power. This is a statement that precisely fits the idea of people being open to the presence of the Holy Spirit and the gifts of the Spirit. The modern church and Paul are in many ways representative of mindsets from opposite ends of the scale, one embraces intellectualism, with its focus on ideas, not actions. The power mindset of St. Paul seeks genuine transformation on an international scale. It all begins with humans being open to enabling the Spirit of God to transform them.

Chapter Fourteen

St. John and Greek thought

In chapter 3 of this book, we looked at 1 John and how St. John wrote about deception in the church. That deception was Gnosticism which is a heresy that is derived from Greek thought. Chapter 3 discusses strategies to define and identify deception. This chapter extends the discussion regarding the contrast between Greek v Hebrew thought.

14.1 The 1 John Teaching about Serious Deception

This specific account of deception in the Bible begins in 1 John 2, and the first part of the detailed discussion begins in 1 John 2:18-20.

1 John 2:18 Children, it is the last hour [the end of this age]; and just as you heard that the antichrist is coming [the one who

will oppose Christ and attempt to replace Him], even now many antichrists (false teachers) have appeared, which confirms our belief that it is the last hour.

1 John 2:19 They went out from us [seeming at first to be Christians], but they were not really of us [because they were not truly born again and spiritually transformed]; for if they had been of us, they would have remained with us; but they went out [teaching false doctrine] so that it would be clearly shown that none of them is of us.

1 John 2:20 But you have an anointing from the Holy One [you have been set apart, specially gifted and prepared by the Holy Spirit], and all of you know [the truth because He teaches us, illuminates our minds, and guards us against error]. AMP

This was initially discussed in chapter 3. This deception was initially found in a group of people who originally belonged to the church and seemed to be genuine disciples. According to the Amplified version, they went out and taught a false doctrine. Given that it was a teaching issue, it is reasonable to assume it would be detected as a teaching issue. Despite this reasonable assumption, this problem was not detected intellectually. The anointing of the Holy Spirit was the key to identifying this deception.

14.2 What do we Know about this Deception?

The deceived ones were initially found within the church. This means they were not against being part of the church and they probably claimed to be Christian despite the fact they believed in false doctrine. They had come under the influence of the spirits of the antichrist. According to the Amplified Bible version of 1 John 2:19 they were not truly born again or spiritually transformed. One could conclude from this they were still thinking in a non-spiritual or fleshy/natural way.

The factor that separated these false believers and the true believers was the anointing of the Holy One, or in the words of the KJV version, the unction from the Holy One.

1 John 2:20 But you have an anointing from the Holy One [you have been set apart, specially gifted and prepared by the Holy Spirit], and all of you know [the truth because He teaches us, illuminates our minds, and guards us from error]. AMP

1 John 2:20 But ye have an unction from the Holy One, and ye know all things.KJV

On the one hand, they were found within the church even though they were "not truly born again and spiritually transformed" as per the Amplified version of 1 John 2:19. The key to avoiding this deception was the presence of the Holy Spirit.

14.3 The Problem was a Spiritual One.

The key problem that the commentaries almost universally acknowledge is Gnosticism. John MacArthur writes, " Most likely, John was combating the beginnings of this virulent heresy that threatened to destroy the fundamentals of the faith and the churches ... Gnosticism, influenced by such philosophers as Plato, advocated a dualism asserting that matter was inherently evil and spirit was good. As a result of this presupposition, these false teachers, although attributing some form of deity to Christ, denied his true humanity to preserve him from evil" (210). Let us examine 1 John 4 from the context of Gnosticism. The influence of these Gnostics needs to be tested. The test of 1 John 4 is whether Jesus came in the flesh or not. The spirits of the antichrist deny it, yet those of God confess Jesus came in the flesh.

14.4 The Significance of 1 John 4 part 1

Let's look at 1 John 4:1-3.

1 John 4:1-3: Beloved, do not believe every spirit [speaking through a self-proclaimed prophet]; instead test the spirits to see whether they are from God, because many false prophets and teachers have gone out into the world. 2 By this you know and recognise the Spirit of God: every spirit that acknowledges and confesses [the fact] that Jesus Christ has [actually] come in the flesh [as a man] is from God [God is its source]; 3 and every spirit that does not confess Jesus [acknowledging that He has come in the flesh, but would deny any of the Son's true nature] is not of God; this is the spirit of the antichrist, which you have heard is coming and is now already in the world.

The Gnostic heresy adopts the Platonic belief that all flesh is evil. So according to the Gnostic view, Jesus cannot be human, or this would, by the Gnostic understanding, mean that he is evil. One early form of Gnosticism is Docetism, which believes Jesus cannot have a body. There are other forms of Gnosticism, all of which agree that Jesus could not be born human. Considering the devastation that Gnosticism brought to the church it is surprising this account is not more discussed.

The important aspect of Jesus needing to be "in the flesh" is mentioned in Romans 8: 3 to 4.

Rom 8:3-4 For what the Law could not do [that is, overcome sin and remove its penalty, its power] being weakened by the flesh [man's nature without the Holy Spirit], God did: He sent His own Son in the likeness of sinful man as an offering for sin. And He condemned sin in the flesh [subdued it and overcame it in the person of His own Son], [Lev_7:37] 4 so that the [righteous and just] requirement of the Law might be fulfilled in us who do not live our lives in the ways of the flesh [guided by worldliness and our sinful nature], but [live our lives] in the ways of the Spirit [guided by His power]. AMP

Just it was necessary for Jesus to come in the flesh, or else Jesus would not come in the likeness of a man as required by Romans 8:3. And to paraphrase the key points in Romans 8:4 Jesus overcame the sin of the flesh in the power of the Spirit. This means the Greek idea that human flesh is cannot be influenced by the spirit is wrong for those in Jesus. This idea is unbiblical as when God created man He called him good as can be read in Genesis 1:31 and the Gnostic idea places a barrier between the spiritual realm and mankind that doesn't exist according to this verse.

Genesis 1:31: God saw everything that He had made, and behold, it was very good and He validated it completely. And there was evening and there was morning, the sixth day. AMP

The Greek idea of the evil nature of man is the thinking that influenced Augustine and Calvin when they wrote about the sinfulness of mankind. But the fact that this is simply not true is confirmed in 1 John 4.

If Jesus came as a man then, for many, it raises a critical question. How then did the Jesus of the flesh Jesus perform the miracles? If he was acting as the Son of God then Gnostics believe there could be no human element involved in his life, and people could argue that he did the miracles because he was the Son of God. We could also say, as a matter of logic and deduction, that it would be impossible for us as normal human beings to perform miracles. This fits closely to the Cessationist view, and according to 1 John 4:1-3, this is also the belief system that comes from the spirit of the antichrist.

So on one hand we have Cessationism and the spirit of the antichrist denying the ability of believers to flow in the anointing. This is opposite to the way of God. Again, the logic of Gnosticism, Greek thinking and the Enlightenment and Cessationism are all diametrically opposed to biblical truth. At this stage, that biblical truth is simply the ability of mankind to flow with the presence of the anointing and our humanity is not a barrier in itself.

14.5 Jesus and the Anointing for Miracles

The biblical approach repeatedly states that Jesus came in the flesh. So then, how is it possible for Jesus to do the miracles? The key is in the name and definition of the Messiah. The word Christ means anointed one, and this actually defines the Messiah. As it says in Isaiah 11:1-5, the Spirit of the Lord resting upon him is part of the definition of the Messiah.

Isaiah 11:1 Then a Shoot (the Messiah) will spring from the stock of Jesse [David's father], And a Branch from his roots will

bear fruit. 2 And the Spirit of the LORD will rest on Him--
The Spirit of wisdom and understanding, The Spirit of counsel
and strength, The Spirit of knowledge and of the [reverential and
obedient] fear of the LORD-- 3 And He will delight in the fear
of the LORD, And He will not judge by what His eyes see, Nor
make decisions by what His ears hear; 4 But with righteousness
and justice He will judge the poor, And decide with fairness for
the downtrodden of the earth and He shall strike the earth with
the rod of His mouth, And with the breath of His lips He shall
slay the wicked. 5 And righteousness will be the belt around His
loins, And faithfulness the belt around His waist. AMP.

This understanding is extended in Isaiah 61:1 to 3, which is the
Scripture Jesus read in the temple in Luke 4:16-21.

Isaiah 61:1 The Spirit of the Lord GOD is upon me Because the
LORD has anointed and commissioned me to bring good news to
the humble and afflicted; He has sent me to bind up [the wounds
of] the brokenhearted, To proclaim release [from confinement
and condemnation] to the [physical and spiritual] captives And
freedom to prisoners, 2 To proclaim the favourable year of the
LORD, And the day of vengeance and retribution of our God,
To comfort all who mourn, 3 To grant to those who mourn in
Zion the following: To give them a turban instead of dust [on their
heads, a sign of mourning], The oil of joy instead of mourning,
The garment [expressive] of praise instead of a disheartened spirit.
So they will be called the trees of righteousness [strong and magnif-
icent, distinguished for integrity, justice, and right standing with
God], The planting of the LORD, that He may be glorified. AMP.

The fulfilment was in Luke 4:16-21.

Luke 4:16 So He came to Nazareth, where He had been brought up; and as was His custom, He entered the synagogue on the Sabbath, and stood up to read. 17 The scroll of the prophet Isaiah was handed to Him. He unrolled the scroll and found the place where it was written, [Isaiah_61:1-2] 18 "THE SPIRIT OF THE LORD IS UPON ME (the Messiah), BECAUSE HE HAS ANOINTED ME TO PREACH THE GOOD NEWS TO THE POOR. HE HAS SENT ME TO ANNOUNCE RELEASE (pardon, forgiveness) TO THE CAPTIVES, AND RECOVERY OF SIGHT TO THE BLIND, TO SET FREE THOSE WHO ARE OPPRESSED (downtrodden, bruised, crushed by tragedy), 19 TO PROCLAIM THE FAVORABLE YEAR OF THE LORD [the day when salvation and the favour of God abound greatly]." [Isaiah_61:1-2] 20 Then He rolled up the scroll [having stopped in the middle of the verse], gave it back to the attendant and sat down [to teach]; and the eyes of all those in the synagogue were [attentively] fixed on Him. 21 He began speaking to them: "Today this Scripture has been fulfilled in your hearing and in your presence."

Jesus himself announced in Luke 4:21 that he was fulfilling Isaiah 61:1-2 which was the Scripture he read. In this fulfilment, the purpose of the Spirit upon Jesus confirmed he was the Messiah and it provided the anointing for him to preach the good news to the poor. His public ministry began at this point, with the anointing and the presence of the Spirit as defined by Luke 4:18-19.

Prior to the presence of this anointing in Luke 4, Jesus did no miracles. This dovetails back into 1 John 4: 1-3 where Jesus came as a man and was enabled to perform miracles by the anointing of the Spirit of God upon him. This is precisely the significance of 1 John 4:1-3. The understanding that Jesus came in the flesh as a human and he was able to do the miracles makes a statement about us and our capacity as human beings. Our humanity does not automatically prohibit us from doing miracles in the sense that the anointing and power of God can work through humans.

There are multiple pieces of evidence in Scripture that point to the importance of spirituality. Jesus came in the flesh and he showed us how it is possible for those in the flesh to release miracles. Far from denying the possibility of others performing miracles, he encouraged the disciples to do so. In Matthew 10:1 Jesus gave authority to the disciples to pray for the sick.

Matthew 10:1 And when He had called His twelve disciples to Him, He gave them power over unclean spirits, to cast them out, and to heal all kinds of sickness and all kinds of disease. NKJV

Those who ascribe to the belief of Cessationism would say that this healing power ended with the disciples or close to that, yet that is not what Jesus said. In John 14:12 He said.

12 "Most assuredly, I say to you, he who believes in Me, the works that I do he will do also; and greater works than these he will do, because I go to My Father. NKJV

This is a statement for anyone who believes and Jesus places no time limitation on this belief. The only necessary element is belief. This exposes the satanic underbelly of Cessationism. Another interesting part of this Scripture is what follows in John 14 verse 13.

John 14:13 And whatever you ask in My name, that I will do, that the Father may be glorified in the Son.NKJV.

These miracles bring glory to our Heavenly Father. This is a fundamental objective of the Christian life, to bring glory to God.

14.6 The significance of 1 John 4 part 2

Returning to 1 John 4:1-3, we can read that God wants us to confess that Jesus came as a man. The significance of this is that Jesus showed us that we could be a creature of the flesh and receive the anointing. This makes it possible to do miracles and flow in the Spirit. When we look at 1 John 4:4 as the context, the point becomes even clearer.

1 John 4:4 says that you are of God, little children, and have overcome them because He who is in you is greater than he who is in the world. NKJV.

One interesting aspect of these verses is that John is telling us that the spirit of the antichrist wants to say Jesus came as a spiritual entity, not in the flesh. (1 John 4:2). If Jesus came as a spiritual entity he could not teach people, by example, how to flow in the things of the Holy Spirit. In 1 John 2, we know that those influenced by this antichrist spirit were not born again. We also know they were comfortable in church and did not outright deny Jesus. We also know that they did not flow in the anointing and were open to deception.

When we look at 1 John 4:4 we see the context. The context means the anointing of God or greater is He that is in me that He that is in the world. The context speaks of the anointing and validates the idea that these spirits of the antichrist are actively seeking to deny the possibility that humans can be anointed by the Spirit of God.

When we look at the word "anti" it means to oppose or to replace Christ. Christ actually means the anointed one. The etymological perspective explains that the central purpose of the antichrist spirit is to oppose the anointed one or as 1 John 4 teaching shows us this spirit wants to reinterpret Jesus as if he came without an anointing.

14.7 Spirituality and the Anointing

Isaiah 61 starts with "The Spirit of the Lord GOD is upon me, Because the LORD has anointed and commissioned me". This is effectively saying the reason that the Spirit of God rested upon Jesus was to perform the miracles that are listed later. Effectively, it was because of the anointing/presence of the Holy Spirit that Jesus was able to do miracles. Isaiah 61 then lists the tasks that the Spirit will fulfil. They include bringing good news to the humble and afflicted; binding up the wounds of the brokenhearted, and to proclaim release to the physical and spiritual captives. The end result of this anointing is explained in verse 3. It starts with the release of the oil of joy which causes mourning to be replaced by the garment of praise instead of a disheartened spirit and this culminates in God's people being called trees of righteousness and the planting of the LORD. The end result is that God can be glorified. The pathway of miracles to glory is again confirmed.

14.8 Spirits of Antichrist

What 1 John 4 tells us is the spirits of the antichrist want us
to believe that Jesus came without flesh. It is implied he was only
a spiritual being. As a consequence, this spirit is saying it would
be impossible for beings of the flesh, or humanity, to receive the
anointing. In 1 John 2, we learn from the Amplified version that
those influenced by this antichrist spirit were not born again or
spiritually mature. We also know they were comfortable in church
and did not outright deny Christianity, however, these people did
not flow in the anointing and were open to deception.

From the perspective of word meanings antichrist fits the idea of
being opposed to the anointing. In both 1 John 2 and 1 John 4:4
there is a specific discussion about the anointing.

Similarly, in 1 John 2, there is a discussion of the anointing
which is rejected by those influenced by the spirit of the antichrist.
When we look at the name anti means to oppose or to replace
and the word Christ means anointing so from an etymological
perspective it means the spirit opposed to the anointing.

The historical context of 1 John is that it is written to counter
Gnosticism which is a belief system that argues all material things
are evil. This means humans are evil and cannot have the Spirit
of God within us. This is because, according to Gnosticism, the
material world is evil and humans share that evil.

The verses in 1 John said those evil spirits existed when John
wrote and there is no reason to think that they have gone away.
John saw this spirit as being behind deception and false prophecy

(1 John 4:1). It was so significant it is the only demonic spirit spoken about in 1 John. The result according to our previous discussion is that it discourages people from receiving the anointing of the Holy Spirit.

The logical conclusion to John's line of reasoning is that we should embrace the anointing. In addition, we should rejoice in the fact that greater is He that is in me than he who is in the world. This anointing and the resulting ability to do miracles is to be embraced.

Jesus encouraged his disciples to do miracles, and he marvelled at the faith of the Centurion which helped create a miracle (Luke 7:9-10)

Luke 7:9 When Jesus heard these things, He marvelled at him, and turned around and said to the crowd that followed Him, "I say to you, I have not found such great faith, not even in Israel!" 10 And those who were sent, returning to the house, found the servant well who had been sick. (NKJV)

Conversely, Jesus was angry with his disciples when they could not heal the boy with epilepsy. He called them a faithless and perverse generation.

Luke 9:38-42. 38 Suddenly a man from the multitude cried out, saying, "Teacher, I implore You, look on my son, for he is my only child. 39 And behold, a spirit seizes him, and he suddenly cries out; it convulses him so that he foams at the mouth; and it departs from him with great difficulty, bruising him. 40 So I implored Your disciples to cast it out, but they could not." 41 Then Jesus answered and said, "O faithless and perverse generation, how long shall I be with you and bear with you? Bring your son here." 42 And as he was still coming, the demon threw him down and convulsed him.

Then Jesus rebuked the unclean spirit, healed the child, and gave him back to his father. (NKJV)

We see in these two verses a clear contrast. Jesus loved the faith that brought miracles, and he hated the lack of faith that would leave a boy unwell. Jesus expected his disciples to have spiritual authority. As we have seen in John 14:12 Jesus expects that even believers should have the faith to heal.

This spirit of antichrist is behind the deception that stops people from believing it is possible and/or desirable for them to have the anointing. This spirit also wants to block us from understanding that greater is He inside the believer than he that is in this world. What this means is that there is a deceptive spiritual force that has its roots in Greek thinking and to this day seeks to deny the capacity that Jesus created for his believers to flow with the anointing of the Holy Spirit.

For those who would wish to argue that anointing is different from being born again, I would agree with you. The anointing comes when we pray for spiritual gifts and it does not, of necessity, come to every believer. There are those who would rightly point out that in the Old Testament dispensation the anointing oil was only given to kings and priests. The wonderful thing about the blood of Jesus is that it brings more that simply salvation. The full dimensions of what the blood brings are beyond the scope of this book as the blood initiated all of the new covenants. As it says in Revelation 1:5-6, the blood of Jesus has made us kings and priests unto God.

Revelation 1:5 And from Jesus Christ, who is the faithful witness, and the first begotten of the dead, and the prince of the kings

of the earth. Unto him, that loved us, and washed us from our sins
in his own blood,

6 And hath made us kings and priests unto God and his Father;
to him be glory and dominion forever and ever. Amen.

We see again this miraculous provision that makes us kings and
priests comes with a reference to both the Glory and dominion of
God. As we exercise the authority of these offices and bring blessings to the world, God is glorified and his dominion is extended.

The Hebrew understanding seeks intimacy with the Spirit of
God and that brings with it the anointing of God. As Paul said,
I come not is the wisdom of man but the power of God. These are
clear biblical values. It is important that we strip away the influence
of Greek thought that has for centuries led the church away from
intimacy with God.

John is effectively arguing in 1 John that there are demonic forces
(known as the spirits of the antichrist) and we should test every
spirit so we to avoid them. One of the end goals of that spirit is to
stop humanity from being anointed. This contrasts with the Spirit
of God that wants us to be anointed and wants us to be full of
the Holy Spirit. Further, we should rejoice because the greater one
lives in us. Jesus said "seek ye first the kingdom of God, and his
righteousness" and then in Paul; and all these things shall be added
unto you. Then in 1 Corinthians 4:20, we learn that the kingdom
of God is not based on talk but on power.

When we add these two verses together, we get a clear message to
make the search for righteousness and the power of God our first
priority. What John is effectively saying in 1 John 4 is that when
this search for the power of God (as exemplified in the anointing)
is encouraged, then you have a true prophet and teacher. The con-

trast to false teachers and prophets is that they argue that humanity is too sinful to receive the anointing, and this search is effectively discouraged. This also aligns with what Paul says in 2 Tim 3:5 where people who adopt a false (or so-called) religion deny the power. The power and the presence of The Holy Spirit create that power that is the benchmark of being biblical.

When we put aside Greek thinking, as it relates to the things of God, we embrace the intimacy with God that Hebrew thinking brings. It is then axiomatic that we will begin to embrace the Spirit of God and the power that it brings. Part of the sacrifice of Jesus was to make us kings and priests, as well as to make a path for the Spirit of God to live within us. The contrast between the intimacy of Hebrew thinking, and the distance that comes with Greek thinking, really sets the ground rules for the way we approach God.

These verses show that the church has fallen into serious deception and there is a reason for it. We all face spiritual opposition that is emboldened when we start to do things with our own strength. There are spiritual forces that encourage a form of religion that is powerless. This is what comes when we seek to do things in our human, albeit fleshy, capacities.

To develop the Spirit of God within us requires initial repentance followed by a cultivation of the fruits of the Spirit, as in Galatians 5:22-24. The challenges of the world as it approaches the second coming should encourage us to embrace the Holy Spirit as never before. Putting aside Greek intellectualism is the first step to breaking long-entrenched spiritual strongholds.

Chapter Fifteen

Greek and Hebrew thought and their Influence

15.1 Summing up the Influence of Greek Thought.

There is a consistent influence that Greek thinking brings: The Hebrew view is an alternative to Greek thinking. After reading this book until now, I hope the need for the church to return to true spirituality should be obvious.

It starts with separation often combined with ideas like the unknowability of God and God's inability to perform miracles.

There is a consistent pattern, Greek thought always starts by seeking to make God distant and unknowable with specific variations.

The most influential Greek thinker in this area is Plato. Plato emphasised the separation between the intellectual/spiritual world of the forms and the depravity of mankind.

This separation continued with Philo, who was the first to integrate Greek thought and Christianity. (refer to section 7.3) The first idea Philo taught was the distant nature and the incomprehensibility of The Christian God. Philo died in 50 AD. Plotinus continued the development of Neo-Platonism till 269 AD and he argued that God's existence is so transcendent and incomprehensible that Neo-Platonism has no concept of a personal God.

Paul constantly emphasises the power of God and the tension it has with Greek thought.

John shows how the spirit of the antichrist wants us to be a people without an anointing But the Spirit of God wants everyone to be anointed.

We see this lack of spirituality with the influence of:

The early version of Apollos

The Gnostics

Augustine

Calvin

Jesus, when the Creeds interpret Him.

The academic world in general (there are exceptions).

The common thread is that the power of the Holy Spirit is absent. It shouldn't be surprising this is what you should expect when people try to do things from their own capabilities, As N.T .Wright argues, many versions of current Christianity are close to Deism, which means spirituality is close to non-existent. (213)

15.2 Summing up the Influence of Hebrew Thought.

Hebrew thought centres on what Jesus gave to mankind.

This is the faith of miracles as expressed by:

The Jesus that the Creeds ignore

Jesus and his desire to bring humans into intimacy with God and spirituality.

The power of Paul and his desire that we understand spiritually.

John the apostle's desire for all to be spiritual and that greater be inside them than He who is in the world.

As we want to be Biblical it is good to remember that according to John 3:3 and Ephesians 1:13, where both argue, in their own way, that we are not actually Christians unless the Holy Spirit lives within us. It is the presence of the Holy Spirit that proves that our faith is genuine. What people with our modern western mindset would describe as spirituality was simply part of the world and life experience of the Hebrew people.

15.3 Leaving Greek-Corrupted Faith Behind

The only path to becoming more Biblical is to develop intimacy with God.

Intimacy is God's idea and comes when we respond to how much God loves us and has good plans for us.

At every turn, western Christianity has been limited by the mindset which comes from Greek thinking.

As we seek the presence of the Holy Spirit, our values become re-aligned according to these words of Jesus. But seek first his kingdom and his righteousness, and all these things will be given to you as well. (Matthew 6:33)

In the final sections, I will examine ways we can develop this focus of seeking God

Chapter Sixteen

Where Hebrew Thinking Leads

In this Chapter, I will suggest some of the consequences that will occur when churches start to embrace the Hebrew thoughts of Jesus, Paul and John. The end goal is to understand the heart of God and to realign the church to what the Bible intended. But the church is ultimately made up of human beings with all that comes with our potential and our limitations. Traditional thinking tends to focus on the need for repentance. While there is a place for that Colossians makes a number of amazing promises.

16. 1 Understanding the Heart of God

First, in Colossians 1:13. it is promised that Christians are moved from the power of darkness to God's kingdom.

Colossians 1:13: He has delivered us from the power of darkness and conveyed *us* into the kingdom of the Son of His love, NKJV

Then in Colossians 1:19-20, we are told that the fullness dwells in Jesus and He has reconciled everything to Himself.

Colossians 1:19-20 For it pleased *the Father that* in Him all the fullness should dwell, **20** and by Him to reconcile all things to Himself, by Him, whether things on earth or things in heaven, having made peace through the blood of His cross.

In Colossians 1:22 the reconciliation which comes through his body sees us as holy and blameless.

Colossians 1:22. in the body of His flesh through death, to present you holy, and blameless, and above reproach in His sight— NKJV

Then In Colossians God wants to reveal the riches in glory which is Jesus within us.

Colossians 1:27 To them God willed to make known what are the riches of the glory of this mystery among the Gentiles: which is Christ in you, the hope of glory. NKJV

While repentance is appropriate when we are part of the kingdom of darkness, the plan of our Heavenly Father is to move us to something different. It is to move us to something different. When we start to see ourselves through the eyes of our Heavenly Father who we are now changes. But just as importantly who we can become changes.

When the church learns to put aside the incessant criticism of our humanity that Greek dualism brings we can start to see ourselves us as our Heavenly Father sees us.

When we as a church can understand how much we are loved and the riches in glory that God destines within us. His personal knowledge of each of us has different plans and brings new and different capabilities, How can anyone deny the possibilities of this of us that have the Holy Spirit living within us? Yes if we need to repent do that, but let's start to focus not on our human limitations but on the possibilities that God wants to bring to our lives.

16.2 Understanding the God within

Our Heavenly Father's desire to dwell with us, and the concept of tabernacling with His people, is recorded as far back as what He told Moses in Exodus 25:8:

Exodus 25:8 " Have them build a sanctuary for Me, so that I may dwell among them" AMP

His actual desire for fellowship is the reason he created men and women and then in John 1:14, there is a description of Jesus as the Word made flesh coming to live with his people.

John 1:14: And the Word became flesh and dwelt among us, and we beheld His glory, the glory as of the only begotten of the Father, full of grace and truth. NKJV.

The word dwell/dwelt in John 1:14 is G4637 in the Strong's concordance plus this word reveals there are implied references to the tabernacle of old. (214)

God's desire is to be with his people. It is interesting that unlike the cathedrals of today, the early tabernacle on the outside appeared to be just a tent. Jesus himself was described in Isaiah 53:2 as having no form or comeliness. In other words, he was not a handsome man. There are many details regarding the building of the tabernacle as can be seen in the chapters after Exodus 25:1.

These chapters speak with detail about what is inside the temple, and many of them speak prophetically of Jesus.

Then in Ezekiel 36:26, the words of Scripture move to a prophetic foretelling of the release of the Holy Spirit, God promises us a heart of flesh and in verse 37, this is God's promise to put his Spirit within us. These verses describe the presence of the Holy Spirit within us and reflect God's desire to be close to His people. This is the reality of our heavenly Father. He is more than just an entity to be known intellectually. He wants to be close to us and bless us. As we learn about Hebrew thinking the intensity of the passion behind these ideas will start to be better known, The sad sight of large groups of people claiming allegiance to Jesus, yet not opening themselves up to the presence of God will hopefully start to be just a memory. But in addition, those churches that do believe in the presence of the Spirit of God are called to explore the reality of the glory that lies within. This is all Biblical according to Colossians 1 but far from living that reality today.

16.3 Understanding the God of True Prophecy

I hope that this connection with the presence of God will help people to hear Him clearly, Also, there is more to this than God dwelling in us for sake of the connection. It is also the beginning of God's plan to partner with his people. When God partners with his people the presence of the Spirit comes and people start to understand God. Many old-time prophecies seemed to me to be critical of people and the prophets themselves seemed to have a harsh demeanour. Greek thinking is similarly critical of people and this is not the Biblical standard.

Right after where Paul encourages all believers to prophesy in 1 Corinthians 14:1 is the verse that specifies that true prophecy is edification, exhortation and comfort.)

1 Corinthians 14: 1-3 Pursue love, and desire spiritual *gifts,* but especially that you may prophesy. 2 or he who speaks in a tongue does not speak to men but to God, for no one understands *him;* however, in the spirit, he speaks mysteries. 3 But he who prophesies speaks edification and exhortation and comfort to men. NKJV

Romans 8:14 includes another statement that touches on relationships.

Romans 8:14 For as many as are led by the Spirit of God, these are sons of God. NKJV

Being a son or daughter of God requires us to be led by God and all this is connected with our relationship and intimacy with God's Spirit. This contrasts with the distant style of faith that is typical of Greek thinking. This distant god-type thinking means people are unsure if God loves them and unsure of His plans for their life. However, when the Spirit of God lives within us there is not only the power of the overcomer. as per 1 John 4:4, but also the assurance that the presence of God brings.

1 John 4:4 You are of God, little children, and have overcome them because He who is in you is greater than he who is in the world NKJV

These verses show that God wants to give his children revelation and authority. These are all parts of revelation that give us clues to understand the kingdom of God.

When we understand how much the Hebrew-thinking God loves us the idea of prophecy becomes much more attractive.

16.4 Removing ourselves from Greek thinking

There are many differences between the Greek Gods and our Heavenly Father. The Greek god Zeus was full of thunder and lightning, whereas our Heavenly Father is described as being full of love and this can be seen in the person of Jesus. Unlike Zeus, God is not full of wrath and anger, waiting to destroy His own. These Greek Gods are impersonal and distant and the claim that God loves us is disputed by people influenced by Greek thinking. While God is Holy and righteous, his desire is to be with us. This is reflected in Him setting up the tabernacle in the desert, it is reflected in the way Jesus came to be with us and it is reflected in the way He sent His Spirit to live in us. The Greek way of thinking leads people to think God is distant. However, God is seeking that last lamb even when the ninety-nine is safe. If God is in total control, then the logical human response is to be passive. Why should you do anything when God has it all in control anyway? Re-enforcing this idea of control is the Greek thought that all material, including mankind, is evil. The Greek idea is that not only is God in control, but we are wretches and profound sinners. The idea we can change the world for the better could be nothing but human arrogance. Dualism is where things or ideas are divided into categories. Examples are the divide between sacred and profane, the divide between work and worship, and finally the spiritual and the natural. God has sent his Holy Spirit and the Spirit is central to bringing God's kingdom to earth. The history of the Welsh revival reveals that prayer can be incredibly powerful. As 2 Corinthians 4:4 says: As we have read Paul wanted everyone to prophesy in 1 Corinthians 14: 5In Matthew 28:18 Jesus speaks of having all authority. It changes the way we see ourselves as we begin to understand we are really loved. It changes our perspective because He is a God that wants to answer our prayers. No longer should we consider ourselves helpless as we have read in John 14:12 that we have the potential to do greater things than Jesus. As Jesus said in Matthew 19:26: "With men this is impossible, but with God all things are possible."

16.5 Greek thinking and the idea of escape

The Hebrew perspective is again a challenge to our culture's automatic acceptance of Greek thought. One of the most influential concepts based on dualism is what is called the sacred profane divide. Some things are sacred like churches and priests, whereas other things are profane, like other buildings and other jobs. When Christians come to church, the idea is that they left their mundane lives for the splendour of the temple. With it are the art, the sacred objects and the ornate clothes of the temple. This dualism supposedly gives people a taste of heaven before they die. Yet the real taste of heaven comes when God dwells with us. The dualistic thinking of the sacred and profane suggests that the purpose of religious belief is to help us escape the world rather than live within it.

Cathedral mentality -Greek / Tabernacle mentality - Hebrew

Salvation means we are escaping this world so we can live in heaven / God wants to dwell on earth amongst his people

The kingdom of heaven does not exist on this earth / The kingdom of Heaven is God, reign on earth

The goal of the Messiah is to help us escape from earth / The goal of the Messiah is so that we can rule and reign on earth

A church dominated by Greek thought simply wants to escape to heaven. A church that embraces Hebrew thought will understand that the God living within has plans.

Plans like praying for God's kingdom to come and will to be done on earth. These are not just words. In 1 Corinthians 4: 20 we can understand that they mean to bring God's spiritual power to earth.

1 Corinthians 4:20 For the kingdom of God is not in word, but in power. NKJV.

The power of God is central to the Hebrew message. We are not called to just die and go to heaven.

16.6 The Church and Authority

In the Bible, the church is typically described as the ecclesia. According to the online Merriam-Webster dictionary, the definition of the ecclesia is " the periodic meeting of the Athenian citizens for conducting public business and for considering affairs proposed by the council" (215)

This is a decision-making body for public affairs and assumes the church will be an active influence in the local public arena.

The original Greek conception of Ecclesia is consistent with Lance Wallnau and the idea of the church having 7 mountains of influence. The Greek idea is that the church and state are separated.

In 2013 Bill Johnson and Lance Wallnau wrote the book *Invading Babylon: The 7 Mountain Mandate.* This book teaches the details of this idea. (216)

These 7 areas of influence include:

1/ Government

2/ Media

3/ Arts and Entertainment

4/ Business

5/ Education

6/ Religion

7/ Family

Similarly, the Lord is the Lord of Hosts which ties in with Ephesians 6 where in verses 10 and 11 Paul writes:

10 Finally, my brethren, be strong in the Lord and in the power of His might. 11 Put on the whole armour of God, that you may be able to stand against the wiles of the devil. (NKJV)

The imagery of a Christian that Paul is writing about here is based on the description of a Roman soldier of the day. Paul continues in verses 12 and 13:

12 For we do not wrestle against flesh and blood, but against principalities, against powers, against the rulers of the darkness of this age, against spiritual hosts of wickedness in the heavenly places. 13 Therefore take up the whole armour of God, that you may be able to withstand in the evil day, and having done all, to stand. (NKJV)

Yet despite this very clear biblical description of our call to spiritual warfare, the Church, with some notable exceptions, has developed a passive mindset. This contrast between most churches and the biblical mandate seems to only make sense if we understand that we are being opposed by spiritual forces. The Lord of Hosts is one of the dominant understandings that come from the Old Testament and the Kingdom of Heaven dominated much of Jesus' teaching.

Many in the Western world reject the church on the premise that they don't believe a spiritual world exists, let alone a King of the heavenly kingdom. The challenge is there for the church to provide credible evidence of the existence of the supernatural. Understanding Ephesians 6:12 informs us this is not an intellectual challenge, but rather a spiritual one.

Ephesians 6:12 For we do not wrestle against flesh and blood, but against principalities, against powers, against the rulers of the darkness of this age, against spiritual *hosts* of wickedness in the heavenly *places.*

Dr A. T. Pierson once said, "There has never been a spiritual awakening in any country or locality that did not begin in united prayer." (217)

16.7 Prophetic transformation: The lesson of Ezekiel 37.

The world of prophecy does not just include revelation it can also include transformation. In Ezekiel 37 God asks Ezekiel to pray the prayer of God's heart. It was a prophetic declaration designed to create and transform. It is powerful and biblical. When we read the prophetic prayer of Ezekiel, we understand that God wants prophetic people not just to understand but also to transform. It starts with prophetic vision but it leads to prophetic proclamations that are powerful. It is of course important that these prayers reflect what God wants.

This is Ezekiel 37 v1 and 4-14. The hand of the Lord came upon me and brought me out in the Spirit of the Lord, and set me down in the midst of the valley; and it *was* full of bones. .. **4** Again He said to me, "Prophesy to these bones, and say to them, 'O dry bones, hear the word of the Lord! **5** Thus says the Lord God to these bones: "Surely I will cause breath to enter into you, and you shall live. **6** I will put sinews on you and bring flesh upon you, cover you with skin and put breath in you; and you shall live. Then you shall know that I *am* the Lord." ' "

7 So I prophesied as I was commanded; and as I prophesied, there was a noise, and suddenly a rattling; and the bones came together, bone to bone. **8** Indeed, as I looked, the sinews and the flesh came upon them, and the skin covered them over; but *there was* no breath in them.

⁹ Also He said to me, "Prophesy to the breath, prophesy, son of man, and say to the ^jbreath, 'Thus says the Lord God: "Come from the four winds, O breath, and breathe on these slain, that they may live."' " ¹⁰ So I prophesied as He commanded me, and breath came into them, and they lived, and stood upon their feet, an exceedingly great army.

¹¹ Then He said to me, "Son of man, these bones are the whole house of Israel. They indeed say, 'Our bones are dry, our hope is lost, and we ourselves are cut off!' ¹² Therefore prophesy and say to them, 'Thus says the Lord God: "Behold, O My people, I will open your graves and cause you to come up from your graves, and bring you into the land of Israel. ¹³ Then you shall know that I *am* the Lord, when I have opened your graves, O My people, and brought you up from your graves. ¹⁴ I will put My Spirit in you, and you shall live, and I will place you in your own land. Then you shall know that I, the Lord, have spoken *it* and performed *it*," says the Lord.' "

God has given humanity the power to prophetically declare as we can see in this verse. As we speak what is on the heart of God it creates miracles. When people learn how to proclaim what is in the heart of God powerful things can happen.

It is time the church started to pray more prayers that start with that kind of vision. However, please be careful and make sure you are asking for things that God wants. When you start declaring a big ministry for yourself and personal success and personal wealth, be careful. Make sure these things are really from God. Proclaiming things for wrong purposes can stir up witchcraft and control and no one wants that.

16.8 Jesus has the Authority via The Lord's prayer.

Matthew 28:18: And Jesus came and spoke to them, saying, "All authority has been given to Me in heaven and on earth. 19 Go therefore and make disciples of all the nations, baptizing them in the name of the Father and of the Son and of the Holy Spirit, 20 teaching them to observe all things that I have commanded you; and lo, I am with you always, *even* to the end of the age."Amen.

The making of disciples is a function of the authority of Jesus and the role of believers is similarly a function of bringing God's kingdom to earth, which is an act of authority.

The end goal is still expressed by the Lord's prayer.

Matthew 6:9-13:

9: Our Father in heaven, Hallowed be Your name.

10 Your kingdom come. Your will be done On earth as *it is* in heaven.

11 Give us this day our daily bread. 12 And forgive us our debts, As we forgive our debtors.

13 And do not lead us into temptation But deliver us from the evil one. For Yours is the kingdom and the power and the glory forever. Amen.

Spirituality begins with intimacy with God.

For some the path is by prophecy for others it is by prayer.

It continues as we explore the Lord's prayer and develop our spiritual understanding.

For everyone, it is different as our God is a personal God.

We live in a world that has tried to interpret Christianity in a natural way, but there is so much more to it than that.

AS John 14:12 says the miracles of Jesus are for every believer.

John 14:12: "Most assuredly, I say to you, he who believes in Me, the works that I do he will do also; and greater *works* than these he will do, because I go to My Father.

The beginnings of belief start with intimacy and learning who Jesus really is as we separate ourselves from the distortions of Greek thought. The challenge is to really understand spirituality and that part of humanity that has been historically suppressed. As we understand the potential that believers can have these miracles will become more common.

16.9 Listening to God changes Many Things

We have the potential to not only hear directly from God about specific details in our lives, but we have the ability to pray for change. These changes are not without their challenges as we enter into real warfare between spiritual kingdoms and we learn about how God has plans for our life

16.10 Spirituality changes everything

In summary, as we learn to get closer to God it opens up the world of the spiritual. This spiritual world was the bedrock of the ministries of Jesus, Paul and John.

It is this that Paul based his ministry on spiritual power not the wisdom of the world, A ministry that is still reverberating around the world despite the influence of Greek thinking that has sought to repress it.

Hebrew thinking enables us to escape the mindset that says God is distant and there is nothing beyond our physical realm.

Hebrew thinking lets us understand that despite the lies told about Him God really loves us.

Not only that God wants to engage with us in a personal way and help us to be the people we were created to be,

The natural world can be cruel and merciless and there is no doubt that there are spiritual forces that do not have our best interests at heart

Hebrew thinking opens many doors. One of the most important is that God has promised that our prayers can make mountains fall into the sea. Mark 11:22-14.

Mark 11:22-24 So Jesus answered and said to them, "Have faith in God. [23] For assuredly, I say to you, whoever says to this mountain, 'Be removed and be cast into the sea,' and does not doubt in his heart, but believes that those things he says will be done, he will have whatever he says. [24] Therefore I say to you, whatever things you ask when you pray, believe that you receive *them,* and you will have *them.*

This does not mean that everything is easy. The struggle between kingdoms is very real. But people who pray passionately achieve amazing things.

There was George Muller built many orphanages in the UK in the 1800s as a result of prayer. (218)

Then there is the leadership of Martin Luther King and the way he inspired a movement of millions and bought new levels of equality to the United States. (219)

The words of his speeches still resonate as some of the most prophetic words ever spoken.

As we develop intimacy with God we open doors to spirituality. and the potential to really bring the blessings of God.

Chapter Seventeen

A Call to Vision

When we read 1 John 4:1-4, these verses can be seen as a recognition of the beginning of a movement designed to suppress spirituality in the church.

1 John 4:1-4: Beloved, do not believe every spirit, but test the spirits, whether they are of God; because many false prophets have gone out into the world. 2 By this you know the Spirit of God: Every spirit that confesses that Jesus Christ has come in the flesh is of God, 3 and every spirit that does not confess that Jesus Christ has come in the flesh is not of God. And this is the *spirit* of the Antichrist, which you have heard was coming and is now already in the world. 4 You are of God, little children, and have overcome them because He who is in you is greater than he who is in the world.

In the earlier chapters of this book it can be seen that after the first century, the Hebraic approach to God was virtually lost. We also understand that the goal of the spirit of the antichrist is to make people believe it is impossible for them to receive the anointing. But in 1 John 4:4, the receiving of that anointing is encouraged. The influence of Greek thinking has systematically suppressed spirituality in the church for almost two thousand years.

The demonic realm has also made a priority of suppressing spirituality and intimacy with God. As the church renews its intimacy with God Hebraic spirituality will be restored. It is hoped that as the people of God understand the historical events outlined in this book they make a priority of restoring true first-century spirituality. Without spirituality, Christianity is just moral teaching. With spirituality, people become empowered to escape the darkness and really transform lives that have been influenced by darkness.

The desired end result is that people become will become empowered to relate to God and the fact they are loved. This opens up possibilities that are impossible for natural people. It is no wonder preaching about spirituality was such a threat to the world of the first century. It is still a threat. But more importantly, it is the Spirit of God that is the only true hope we have in a world full of darkness.

It is the spirit of God that is essential for the salvation that Jesus described in John 3;3. But the spirit is not just limited to salvation as it includes the full power of Isaiah 61

1-7 and the anointing.

Isaiah 61:1-7. "The Spirit of the Lord God *is* upon Me. Because the Lord has anointed Me To preach good tidings to the poor; He has sent Me to heal the brokenhearted, To proclaim liberty to the captives, And the opening of the prison to *those who are* bound; [2] To proclaim the acceptable year of the Lord, And the day of vengeance of our God; To comfort all who mourn, [3] To console those who mourn in Zion, To give them beauty for ashes,

The oil of joy for mourning, The garment of praise for the spirit of heaviness; That they may be called trees of righteousness, The planting of the Lord, that He may be glorified."

4 And they shall rebuild the old ruins, They shall raise up the former desolations, And they shall repair the ruined cities, The desolations of many generations. **5** Strangers shall stand and feed your flocks, And the sons of the foreigner *Shall be* your ploughmen and your vinedressers. **6** But you shall be named the priests of the Lord, They shall call you the servants of our God. You shall eat the riches of the Gentiles, And in their glory, you shall boast. **7** Instead of your shame *you shall have* double *honor,* And *instead of* confusion, they shall rejoice in their portion. Therefore in their land, they shall possess double; Everlasting joy shall be theirs.

This verse is full of many blessings and every one of them is contingent on the presence of The Spirit.

Jesus said he has been given all authority in heaven and earth. Thinking about this means amazing possibilities when believers receive the anointing and the presence of the Holy Spirit. They are far greater than what most people imagine. I want to encourage people to seek Jesus and the possibilities that come as God releases his latter-day rain as described in Joel 2.

Joel 2:28 "It shall come about after this That I shall pour out My Spirit on all mankind, and your sons and your daughters will prophesy, Your old men will dream dreams, Your young men will see visions. V29 "Even on the male and female servants I will pour out My Spirit in those days. v30 "I will show signs and wonders [displaying My power] in the heavens and on the earth, Blood and fire and Columns of smoke.

It is no accident that the authority and anointing of 1 john 4:4 are written about immediately after 1 John 4:1-3. It is when God's people understand the significance of the fact that the anointing is available to believers. It's time to stop being so influenced by Greek thinking and limiting ourselves to a naturalistic conception of who we are. Born-again humans are also spiritual beings We know that it's not by might or power but by God's Spirit that blessings come. These things have been prophesied a long time ago. We are called to seek the fullness of the Spirit because that's the path to bring the blessings of the kingdom of God to earth. It will take intimacy and prayer, and there are no promises it will be easy, however, God has promised to bless us.

Chapter Eighteen

References

(1) MacCulloch, Diarmaid M (2010). A History of Christianity: The First Three Thousand Years.

(2) Ibid

(3) Gordon, Nehemia (2005) The Hebrew Yeshua vs. the Greek Jesus

(4) https://www.wesleymission.org.au/assets/Documents/ Christian-Life Sermons: What-about-you.pdf

(5) Cambridge Dictionary (2022) Web.https:// dictionary.cambridge.org/english/syncretism

(6) https://chalcedon.edu/magazine/the-danger-of-syncretism

(7) http://bereanassemblyspringhill.org/articles/ the-dangers-of-syncretism/

(8) https://goodfaithmedia.org/ syncretism-not-new-to-christianity-cms-364/

(9) Kraft, Charles. (1990) Christianity with Power.

(10) Ibid

(11) Hopkins, Richard R. (1999) How Greek Philosophy Corrupted the Christian Concept of God.

(12) Ibid

(13) MacArthur, John (2010) The MacArthur Study Bible,

(14) Derickson, Gary W. (2014) The 1, 2, & 3 John: Evangelical Exegetical Commentary.

(15) Ibid

(16) Ibid

(17) MacArthur, John (2010) The MacArthur Study Bible,

(18) Derickson, Gary W. (2014) The 1, 2, & 3 John: Evangelical Exegetical Commentary

(19)MacArthur, John (2010) The MacArthur Study Bible,

(19) https://maninthemirror.org/2008/06/09/ teach-your-men-about-the-bible/

(20) Joyner, Rick. Shadows of Things to Come.

(21) Wright, N.T. (2012) N.T. Wright at Calvin College January Series: God is a Theocrat, and we are his priests

(22) Ibid

(23) Ibid

(24) Ibid

(25) Ibid

(26) Ibid 58:4

(27) Ibid 59:35

(28) Ibid

(29) Taylor, Charles (2007) A Secular Age

(30) Frame, Tom (2009) Losing My Religion.

(31) Maltz, Steve. (2009) How the Church Lost the Way: And How it Can Find it Again.

(32) Ibid

(33) Ibid

(34) Ibid

(35) Ibid

(36) https://www.wildbranch.org/teachings/hebrew-greek-mind/

(37) https://www.thattheworldmayknow.com/hellenism-center-of-the-universe

(38) MacGrath, Alister, E. (2016), Christian Theology, An Introduction.

(39) Maltz, Steve. (2009) How the Church Lost the Way: And How it Can Find it Again.

(40) https://www.worldhistory.org/article/61/protagoras-of-abdera-of-all-things-man-is-the-measure/

(41) https://www.thattheworldmayknow.com/hellenism-center-of-the-universe

(42) Kleinman, Paul.(2013) Philosophy 101: From Plato and Socrates to Ethics and Metaphysics, an Essential Primer on the History of Thought.

(43) https://iep.utm.edu/plato/

(44) Magee, Bryan. (2016) The Story of Philosophy

(45) Ibid

(46) Ibid p.30.

(47) Ibid

(48) Olson, Roger (1999) The Story of Christian Theology

(49) https://www.thattheworldmayknow.com/hellenism-center-of-the-universe

(50) Ibid

(51) Magee, Bryan. (2016) The Story of Philosophy.

(52) Kleinman, Paul.(2013) Philosophy 101

(53) Magee, Bryan. (2016) The Story of Philosophy

(54) Kleinman, Paul.(2013) Philosophy 101

(55) Ibid

(56) Magee, Bryan. (2016) The Story of Philosophy.

(57) Kleinman, Paul.(2013) Philosophy 101: From Plato and Socrates to Ethics and Metaphysics, an Essential Primer on the History of Thought.

(58) Ibid

(59) Olson, Roger (1999) The Story of Christian Theology p. 264

(60)Ibid

(61) Magee, Bryan. (2016) The Story of Philosophy

(62) Kleinman, Paul.(2013) Philosophy 101

(63) https//iep.utm.edu/aristotle/

(64) https://www.patheos.com/blogs/anxiousbench/2015/02/ gnostics-and-platonists

(65)Helleman, Wendy E. (2016) The "Triumph" of Hellenization in Early Christianity

(66) Helleman, Wendy E. (2016) The "Triumph" of Hellenization in Early Christianity

(67) Hengel, Martin (1974) Judaism and Hellenism.

(68) Frost, Michael. (2010) Jesus the Fool.

(69) Hengel, Martin (1974) Judaism and Hellenism p2

(70) Hengel, Martin (1974) Judaism and Hellenism p2

(71) Hengel p2

(72) Hengel p4

(73) Frost, Michael. (2010) Jesus the Fool. Hendrickson Publishers. Peabody. MA.

(74) ibid

(75) ibid

(76) https://www.blueletterbible.org

(77) Frost, Michael. (2010) Jesus the Fool.

(78) Hengel, Martin (1974) Judaism and Hellenism p2

(79) Frend, W.C.H (1984) The Rise of Christianity p35

(80) Hopkins, Richard R. (1999) How Greek Philosophy Corrupted the Christian Concept of God.

(81) Ibid

(82) https://theodora.com/encyclopedia/p2/polycarp.html

(83) Petty, Gary. Plato's Shadow: The Hellenizing of Christianity p. 154

(84) Ibid.

(85) Olson, Roger (1999) The Story of Christian Theology p.84

(86) Petty, Gary. Plato's Shadow: The Hellenizing of Christianity p.158

(87) Hayford, Jack. W. (1984) The Hayford Bible Handbook p. 356

(88) Hopkins, Richard R. (1999) How Greek Philosophy Corrupted the Christian Concept of God.

(89) Olson, Roger (1999) The Story of Christian Theology

(90) Ibid

(91) Petty, Gary. Plato's Shadow: The Hellenizing of Christianity p. 154

(92) Ibid

(93) Ibid

(94) Ibid

(95) Arthur W. Klem, "Tertullian: Victim of Caricature," Bulletin of the Evangelical Theological Society 5.4 (Fall 1962): p. 105.

(96) Ibid p.105

(97) Ibid p.105

(98) Ibid p.105

(99) Petty, Gary. Plato's Shadow: The Hellenizing of Christianity

(100) Ibid p.158

(101) Ibid p.165

(102) Ibid

(103) Hopkins, Richard R. (1999) How Greek Philosophy Corrupted the Christian Concept of God.

(104) Petty, Gary. Plato's Shadow: The Hellenizing of Christianity

(105) Ibid

(106) Ibid

(107) Ibid

(108) Ibid

(109) Magee, Bryan. (2016) The Story of Philosophy p.29

(110) Stanford Encyclopaedia of Philosophy. Article on Saint Augustine by Christian Tourneau.

(111) Magee, Bryan. (2016) The Story of Philosophy p.29

(112) Olson, Roger (1999) The Story of Christian Theology

(113) Ibid

(114) Ibid

(115) Ibid

(116) Ibid

(117) Ibid p. 271

(118) Ibid p. 273

(119) Ibid p.273

(120) Ibid

(121) Ibid

(122) Ibid p. 273

(123) Ibid

(124) Eberle, Harold Christianity unshackled

(125) Ibid p. 47

(126) Ibid

(127) Ibid

(128) Ibid

(129)Johnson, Dru (2019) Did Ancient Hebrews have different minds from the Greeks?

(130) Ibid

(131)) https://ling.yale.edu/about/history/people/ benjamin-lee-whorf

(132))Johnson, Dru (2019) Did Ancient Hebrews have different minds from the Greeks?

(133) Ibid

(134) Barr, James. (1961) The Semantics of Biblical Language.

(135))Johnson, Dru (2019) Did Ancient Hebrews have different minds from the Greeks?

(136) Ibid

(137) Ibid

(138) Ibid

(139) Ibid

(140) Ibid

(141) Barr, James. (1961) The Semantics of Biblical Language.

(142) https://www.independent.co.uk/news/obituaries/ the-rev-professor-james-barr-6230111.html

(143) Barr, James (1993) From Biblical Faith and Natural Theology P.25

(144) Ibid, p.45.

(145) Ibid

(146) Philip King (2010) Surrounded by Bitterness downloaded from https://www.sil.org/resources/archives/9657

(147) https://skipmoen.com/2010/11/james-barr-the-semantics-of-biblical-language/

(148) Ibid

(148) Ibid

(150) Philip King (2010) Surrounded by Bitterness downloaded from https://www.sil.org/resources/archives/9657

(151) Williamson, Hugh. G https://www.independent.co.uk/news/obituaries/the-rev-professor-james-barr-6230111.html

(152) Philip King (2010) Surrounded by Bitterness downloaded from https://www.sil.org/resources/archives/9657

(153) Joosten, Jan Hebrew thought and Greek thought in the Septuagint Fifty years after Barr's Semantics.

(154) Ibid

(155) Ibid

(156) Huxley, Aldous in https://www.philosophicalsociety.com/recentarticles.htm

(157) https://harpers.org/archive/2018/11/a-divine-pat-john-cleese/

(158) Strong's Concordance

(159) https://olivepresspublishers.com/wp/wp-content/uploads/Mind-in-Hebrew-in-Scripture.pdf

(160) Doukhan, Jacques. B, (!993) Hebrew for Theologians p. 194 This comes from 1 kings 19:12.

(161) Tverberg, Lois. Reading the Bible with Rabbi Jesus.

(162) Doukhan, Jacques. B, (!993) Hebrew for Theologians

(163 https://www.pathofobedience.com/words/shama/

(164) Doukhan, Jacques. B, (!993) Hebrew for Theologians

(165) Ibid

(166) Ibid

(167) Ibid

(168) Tverberg, Lois (2017) Reading the Bible with Rabbi Jesus

(169) Doukhan, Jacques. B, (!993) Hebrew for Theologians

(170) Burton, Ernest D. Jesus As a Thinker,

(171) Lewis, Ralph L and Gregg.L, Learning to Preach like Jesus.

(172) Bond, Albert R. , The Master preacher: a study of the homiletics of Jesus.

(173) Ibid.

(174) https://www.growthengineering.co.uk/kolb-experiential-learning-theory/

(175) https://www.growthengineering.co.uk/awards/

(176) Ibid

(177) Grady, Daniel J. A Critical Review of the Application of Kolb's Experiential Learning Theory Applied Through the use of Computer Based Simulations Within Virtual Environments 2000-2016.

(178) Ibid

(179) https://www.questionsgod.com/christian-starter.htm

(180) Burton, Ernest D. Jesus As a Thinker,

(181) Ibid

(182) Tverberg, Lois (2017) Reading the Bible with Rabbi Jesus kindle location 1120/4716

(183) Tverberg, Lois (2017) Reading the Bible with Rabbi Jesus

(184) Barth, Karl (1959) Dogmatics in Outline p31

(185) Herschel, Abraham (1955) God in Search of Man

p. 16, 21.

(186) https://vision.org.au/uncategorized/
home-group-our-undefinable-god/

(187) https://vision.org.au/uncategorized/
home-group-our-undefinable-god/

(188) Tverberg, Lois (2017) Reading the Bible with Rabbi Jesus

(189) Bond,A.R. (1910) The Master preacher: a study of
the homiletics of Jesus. Kindle version. 762/4395

(190) Lewis, Ralph L and Gregg.L, Learning to Preach like Jesus.

p155

(191) Ibid p155

(192) The Stanford Encyclopaedia of Philosophy
https://plato.stanford.edu/entries/logic-inductive/

(193) The Stanford Encyclopaedia of Philosophy
https://plato.stanford.edu/entries/aristotle-logic/

(194) Hill, Wesley, "St. Paul theologian of the trinity"
https://www.firstthings.com/web-exclusives/2012/06/
st-paul-theologian-of-the-trinity Wesley Hill.

(195) Wright, N.T. (2012) N.T. Wright at Calvin College
January Series: God is a theocrat, and we
are his priests (web)

(196) Hayford, Jack. The Hayford Bible Handbook. P354.

(197) Jamieson Faussett Brown volume 3 part 2 p.135
/ Acts 18:24

(198) https://www.britannica.com/topic/rhetoric

(199) Jamieson Faussett Brown commentary
vol 3 part 3 p283 / 1 Corinthians 1:5

(200) Hill, Wesley, "St. Paul theologian of the trinity"

https://www.firstthings.com/web-exclusives/2012/06/
st-paul-theologian-of-the-trinity Wesley Hill.

(201) Ibid

(202) Deissmann, Adolf, (1912) St. Paul a study Social
and Religious History. P.6

(203)Ibid p.6

(204) Ibid p.7

(205) Ibid

(206) A fuller version of Bultmann's quote

"Paul did not theoretically and connectedly develop his
thoughts concerning God and Christ, the world and man in an
independent scientific treatise as a Greek philosopher or a modern
theologian. He only developed them fragmentarily (except in Romans) always broaching them in his letters for a specific and actual
occasion. Even in Romans, where he expressed them connectedly
and with a degree of completeness, he does so in a letter and under
the compulsion of a concrete situation. These facts must not be
allowed to lead one to a false conclusion that Paul was not a real
theologian nor to the notion that to understand his individuality
he must be regarded, instead, as a hero of piety. On the contrary!
The way in which he reduces specific acute questions to a basic
theological question, the way in which he reaches concrete decisions on the basis of fundamental theological considerations,
shows that what he thinks and says grows out of his basic theological position—the position which is more or less completely set
forth in Romans.

Nevertheless, this basic portion is not a structure of theoretical thought. It does not take the phenomena which encounter
man and man himself whom they encounter and build into a

system, a distantly perceived kosmos (system), as Greek science does. Rather, Paul's theological thinking only lifts the knowledge inherent in faith itself into the clarity of conscious knowing. A relation to God that is only feeling, only "piety," and not also knowledge of God and man together is for Paul unthinkable.

The act of faith is simultaneously an act of knowing, and, correspondingly, theological knowing cannot be separated from faith. Therefore, Pauline theology is not a speculative system. It deals with God not as he is in Himself only with God as He is significant for man, for man's responsibility and man's salvation. Correspondingly, it does not deal with the world and man in their relation to God. Every assertion about God is simultaneously an assertion about man and vice versa. For this reason and in this sense Paul's theology is, at the same time, anthropology. (Bultmann 1951, 190- 191)

from Baldwin, Gary Lee, A personality Theory of Christian Spirituality, Winebrenner theological seminary, Ohio USA 2012.

Quoting Bultmann, Rudolf. (1951) Theology of the New Testament, Vol. 1. New York: Charles Scribner's Sons.

(207) Hill, Wesley, "St. Paul theologian of the trinity"

(208) from Baldwin, Gary Lee, A personality Theory of Christian Spirituality, Winebrenner theological seminary, Ohio USA 2012.

Quoting Bultmann, Rudolf. (1951) Theology of the New Testament, Vol. 1. New York: Charles Scribner's Sons.

(209) Wright, N.T. Historical Paul and Systematic theology from https://ntwrightpage.com/2017/02/24/historical-paul-and-systematic-theology

(210) Ibid

(211) Ibid

(212) Olson, Roger (1999) The Story of Christian Theology

(213)Wright, N.T. Historical Paul and Systematic theology from https://ntwrightpage.com/2017/02/24/historical-paul-and-systematic-theology

(214) Strong's Concordance

(215) https://www.merriam-webster.com/dictionary/ecclesia

(216) Johnson, Bill and Wallnau, Lance (2013) Invading Babylon: The 7 Mountain Mandate.

(217) Dr. Peterson, A.T.

(218) Muller, George. (2017) The Autobiography of George Muller.

(219) Hansen, Drew.D.(2005) The Dream.

Chapter Nineteen

Bibliography

Barr, James (1993) *From Biblical Faith and Natural Theology* *Clarendon Press*

Barr, James. (1961) *The Semantics of Biblical Language.*SCM Press, revised edition (2012). London.

Baldwin, Gary Lee, A personality Theory of Christian Spirituality, Winebrenner theological seminary, Ohio USA 2012.

Barth, Karl (1959) Dogmatics in Outline Harper New York:

Bond, Albert R.,(1912) *The Master preacher: a study of the homiletics of Jesus.* New York: American Tract Society. Kindle version.

Burton, Ernest D. *Jesus As a Thinker,*

Bultmann, Rudolf. (1951). Theology of the New Testament, Vol. 1. New York: Charles Scribner's Sons.

Deissmann, Adolf, *(1912) St. Paul a study Social and Religious History,* Hodder and Stoughton London. Forgottenbooks.com *edition*

Derickson, Gary W. (2014) *The 1, 2, & 3 John: Evangelical Exegetical Commentary.* Lexham Press.

Doukhan, Jacques. B, (!993) Hebrew for Theologians

Eberle, Harold (2009) Christianity Unshackled Destiny Image Publishers Shippensburg PA kindle edition

Frame, Tom (2009) *Losing My Religion*. UNSW Press Sydney Australia

Frend, W.C.H (1984) *The Rise of Christianity* Fortress Press.

Frost, Michael. (2010) *Jesus the Fool*. Hendrickson Publishers. Peabody. MA.

Gordon, Nehemia (2005) The Hebrew Yeshua vs. the Greek Jesus, Hilkiah Press

Hayford, Jack. W. (1984) The Hayford Bible Handbook. Thomas Nelson Publis

Helleman, Wendy E. (2016) The "Triumph" of Hellenization in Early Christianity - The Wiley-Blackwell Companion to World Christianity Sanneh/ Wiley.

Hengel, Martin (1974) Judaism and Hellenism. 1981 edition with Fortress Press Philadelphia.

Heschel, Abraham (1955) God in Search of Man   Farrar, Straus & Giroux, New York:

Hopkins, Richard R. (1999) How Greek Philosophy Corrupted the Christian Concept of God. Cedar Fort, Inc.. Kindle Edition.

Jamieson Faussett Brown A Commntary Critical, Experimental, and Practical on the Old and New Testaments.in three volumes reprinted 1978. Eerdmans Grand Rapids Michigan.

Johnson, Bill and Wallnau, Lance (2013) Invading Babylon: The 7 Mountain Mandate. Destiny Image Publishers. Shippensburg, Pennsylvania.

Johnson, Dru (2019) Did Ancient Hebrews have different minds from the Greeks?

Joosten, Jan Hebrew thought and Greek thought in the Septuagint Fifty years after Barr's Semantics.

Joyner, Rick. Shadows of Things to Come. Thomas Nelson. Kindle Edition

Kleinman, Paul.(2013) Philosophy 101: From Plato and Socrates to Ethics and Metaphysics, an Essential Primer on the History of Thought. Adams Media Simon Schuster Sydney NewYork.

Klem, Arthur W. "Tertullian: Victim of Caricature," Bulletin of the Evangelical Theological Society 5.4 (Fall 1962):

Kraft, Charles. (1990) Christianity with Power. Vine Books AnnArbour MI.

Lewis, Ralph L. and Gregg L,. (1989) Learning to Preach like Jesus. 2nd ed. 1982. Crosswayway Books / Good News publishers Whraton Illinois.

MacCulloch, Diarmaid M (2010). A History of Christianity: The First Three   Thousand Years. Penguin Books.

MacArthur, John (2010) The MacArthur Study Bible, Crossway,   Wheaton Illinois.

Magee, Bryan. (2016) The Story of Philosophy. DK Publishing. London.

MacGrath, Alister, E. (2016), Christian Theology, An Introduction.   Wiley- Blackwell. New York

Maltz, Steve. (2009) How the Church Lost the Way: And How it Can Find   it Again. Saffron Planet Publishing UK. Kindle edition.

Olson, Roger (1999) The Story of Christian Theology. Apollos IVP London

Overman, Christian.(2006) Assumptions that Affect our lives. Kindle version.

Petty, Gary. (2013) Plato's Shadow: The Hellenizing of Christianity. Little Frog Publishing. Kindle Edition

Strongs concordance

Taylor, Charles (2007) A Secular Age. The Belknap Press of Harvard University Press, Cambridge, Massachusetts, and London England.

Tverberg, Lois. Reading the Bible with Rabbi Jesus . Baker Publishing Group. Kindle Edition. Location 1135.

Wright, N.T. (2012) N.T. Wright at Calvin College January Series:

Chapter Twenty

Web URLs

https://www.academia.edu/1173650/Hebrew_thought_and_ Greek_thought_in_the_Septuagint_Fifty_years_after_Barr_s _Semantics

http://bereanassemblyspringhill.org/articles/the-dangers-of-syncretism/

https://biblicalstudies.org.uk/pdf/bets/vol05/tertullian_klem. pdf

https://www.blueletterbible.org/search/Dictionary/ viewTopic.cfm?topic=IT0000084,BT0000062

https://www.britannica.com/topic/rhetoric

https://chalcedon.edu/magazine/the-danger-of-syncretism

https://dictionary.cambridge.org/english/syncretism

https://www.firstthings.com/web-exclusives/2012/06/ st-paul-theologian-of-the-trinity

Wesley Hill, "St. Paul theologian of the trinity"

https://www.groupbiblestudy.com/engfire/1.-if-my-people-wh o-are-called.?gclid=Cj0KCQjwxb2XBhDBARIsAOjDZ35HFP

h-l95CmUoUo9KLdU04KEgMkfAwJkzEMPTkN69xJadM4O
yQ_XwaAvQ5EALw_wcB

https://www.growthengineering.co.uk/kolb-experiential-learning-theory

https://www.growthengineering.co.uk/awards/

https://harpers.org/archive/2018/11/a-divine-pat-john-cleese/

https://hebraicthought.org/ancient-hebrews-greeks-minds/#:~
:text=Did%20Ancient%20Hebrews%20Have%20Different%20
Minds%20than%20the%20Greeks%3Fstyle="mso-spacerun:'yes';f
ont-family:'Times New
Roman';mso-fareast-font-family:SimSun;
font-size:12.0000pt;mso-font-kerning:0.0000pt;"

https://iep.utm.edu/aristotle/#:~:text=%E2%80%94322%20B.
C.E.),rejecting%20Plato's%20theory%20of%20forms

https://iep.utm.edu/plato/

https://www.independent.co.uk/news/obituaries/
the-rev-professor-james-barr-6230111.html

https://www.journals.uchicago.edu/doi/abs/
10.1086/472143?mobileUi=0

https://ling.yale.edu/about/history/people/
benjamin-lee-whorf

https://maninthemirror.org/2008/06/09/
teach-your-men-about-the-bible

https://www.merriam-webster.com/dictionary/ecclesia

www.mlive.com/living/grand-rapids/2012/01/
nt_wright_at_calvin_college

https://ntwrightpage.com/2017/02/24/
historical-paul-and-systematic-theology/

https://olivepresspublishers.com/wp/wp-content/uploads/Mind-in-Hebrew-in-Scripture.pdf

https://www.patheos.com/blogs/anxiousbench/2015/02/ gnostics-and-platonists/

https://www.pathofobedience.com/words/shama/

www.philosophicalsociety.com/recentarticles.htm

https://plato.stanford.edu/entries/aristotle-logic/

https://plato.stanford.edu/entries/augustine/

https:// plato.stanford.edu/entries/logic-inductive/

https//www.questionsgod.com/christian-starter.htm

https://www.journals.uchicago.edu/doi/abs/10.1086/472143?mobileUi=0

https://www.sil.org/resources/archives/9657

https://skipmoen.com/2010/11/james-barr-the-semantics-of-biblical-language/

https://www.thattheworldmayknow.com/hellenism-center-of-the-universe

https://theodora.com/encyclopedia/p2/polycarp.html

https:// vision.org.au/uncategorized/home-group-our-undefinable-god/

https://www.wesleymission.org.au/assets/Documents/Christian-Life/Sermons/What-about-you.pdf

https://www.wildbranch.org/teachings/hebrew-greek-mind/

https://www.worldhistory.org/article/61 /protagoras-of-abdera

About the Author

The author of this book is Graeme McLiesh. Graeme is an Australian living in Melbourne. Before writing this book he was an English teacher for International students and a published author. The research paper for his Master's degree was about language learning and was part of an academic compilation. There have also been other books under a pseudonym written as instructional texts for his International English students.

This book "Rediscovering the Heart of God" is the first of what is hoped to be many books written about developing the Hebrew mindset within the church. In this book, Graeme has examined the significance of Hebrew thinking. The church of today is almost singularly the result of Greek thinking. The influence of Greek thought has led many churches to unknowingly present a gospel that differs from the Bible.

This is an academic book that combines a wide range of perspectives. These include the Philosophy and thought analysis that Graeme studied in his BA and the language and historical analysis that Graeme studied in his MA degree in English Language Arts.

This book is more than academic writing, it is also the result of many years of Bible study and prayer. Part of Graeme's dedication to Bible study can be seen in the home groups he has run and the 3 year period he was Associate Pastor of JPA church in Hong Kong. When Graeme started writing in 2020 he did not intend to write a book about the importance of Hebrew thought. However, one morning he felt that this was the book he was supposed to write. As his writing and research continued Graeme continued to receive much spiritual leading. While this book is academic and covers a range of disciplines, Graeme also believes it is a prophetic book as Graeme has been led to write aspects of the book.

The writing process was not quick as much of the book's thinking involves diverse concepts and references. These have been consolidated into a single and coherent piece of writing. As Graeme has been writing this book he has received many ideas for additional books which he plans to write in the future.

For further contact: info@theheartofprophecy.com